Physical Characteristics of the Neapolitan Mastiff

(from the American Kennel Club breed standard)

Back: Wide and strong. Highest part of shoulder blade barely rising above the strong, level topline of the back.

Body: The length of the dog, measured from the point of the shoulder to the point of buttock is 10 to 15 percent greater than the height of the dog measured from the highest point of the shoulder to the ground. Depth of the ribcage is equal to half the total height of the dog. Ribs are long and well sprung.

Croup: Wide, strong, muscular and slightly sloped. The top of the croup rises slightly and is level with the highest point of the shoulder.

Tail: Set on slightly lower than the topline, wide and thick at the root, tapering gradually toward the tip.

Hindquarters: As a whole, they must be powerful and strong, in harmony with the forequarters. Thighs: About the same length as the forearms, broad, muscular. Stifles: Moderate angle, strong. Legs: Heavy and thick boned, well-muscled. Slightly shorter than thigh bones. Hind feet: Same as the front feet but slightly smaller.

Height: Dogs: 26 to 31 inches, Bitches: 24 to 29 inches. Average weight of mature dogs: 150 pounds; bitches: 110 pounds; but greater weight is usual and preferable as long as correct proportion and function are maintained.

Coat: Short, dense and of uniform length and smoothness all over the body. The hairs are straight and not longer than 1 inch. No fringe anywhere.

Color: Solid coats of gray (blue), black, mahogany and tawny, and the lighter and darker shades of these colors.

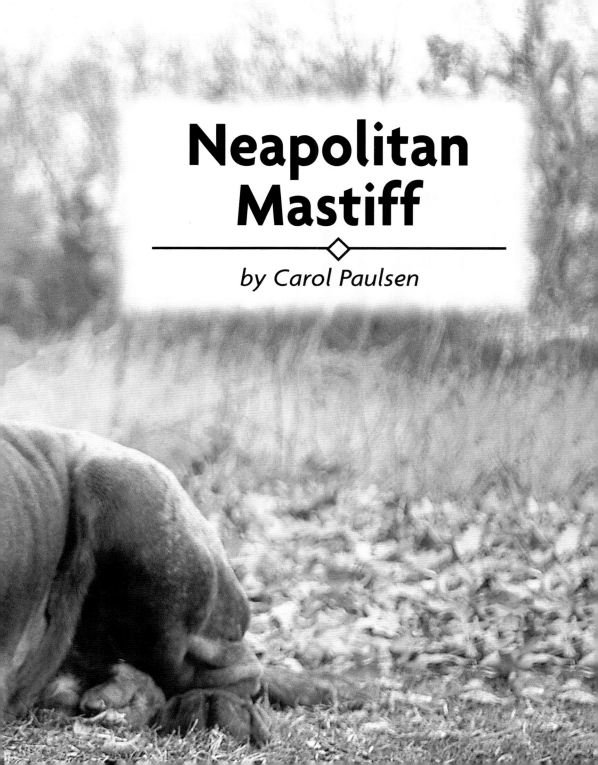

Neapolitan Mastiff

by Carol Paulsen

Contents

9

History of the Neapolitan Mastiff

Developed from hunters and war dogs, and prized for its unique physical characteristics, the Neapolitan Mastiff's real history begins in the Vesuvius region of Italy. Follow the breed from its beginnings as a valued guard dog to its introduction into countries around the world.

16

Characteristics of the Neapolitan Mastiff

The Neapolitan Mastiff is one of the world's most distinct breeds in both looks and personality; learn more about its unique characteristics and find out what makes an ideal Neo owner. Also discussed are breed-specific health considerations of which every new owner should be aware.

28

Breed Standard for the Neapolitan Mastiff

Learn the requirements of a well-bred Neapolitan Mastiff by studying the description of the breed set forth in the Fédération Cynologique Internationale standard. Both show dogs and pets must possess key characteristics as outlined in the breed standard.

34

Your Puppy Neapolitan Mastiff

Be advised about choosing a reputable breeder and selecting a healthy, typical puppy. Understand the responsibilities of ownership, including home preparation, acclimatization, the vet and prevention of common puppy problems.

62

Everyday Care of Your Neapolitan Mastiff

Enter into a sensible discussion of dietary and feeding considerations, exercise, grooming, traveling and identification of your dog. This chapter discusses Neapolitan Mastiff care for all stages of development.

Training Your Neapolitan Mastiff 80

By Charlotte Schwartz
Be informed about the importance of training your Neapolitan Mastiff from the basics of house-training and understanding the development of a young dog to executing obedience commands (sit, stay, down, etc.).

Health Care of Your Neapolitan Mastiff 104

Discover how to select a qualified veterinarian and care for your dog at all stages of life. Topics include vaccination scheduling, skin problems, dealing with external and internal parasites and the eye conditions affecting pure-bred dogs.

Showing Your Neapolitan Mastiff 138

Step into the center ring and find out about the world of showing pure-bred dogs. Here's how to get started in AKC shows, how they are organized and what's required for your dog to become a champion.

Behavior of Your Neapolitan Mastiff 144

Learn to recognize and handle common behavioral problems in your Neo, including aggression with people and other dogs, chewing, barking, mounting, digging, jumping up and more.

Index 156

KENNEL CLUB BOOKS® **NEAPOLITAN MASTIFF**
ISBN: 1-59378-222-5

Copyright © 2003, **2005** • Kennel Club Books, LLC
308 Main Street, Allenhurst, NJ 07711 USA
Cover Design Patented: US 6,435,559 B2 • Printed in South Korea

10 9 8 7 6 5 4 3 2

Photos by:

Norvia Behling, Carolina Biological Supply, Doskocil, Isabelle Francais, James Hayden-Yoav, James R. Hayden, RBP, Carol Ann Johnson, Alice van Kempen, Dwight R. Kuhn

Illustrations by Renée Low.

Special thanks to the owners/breeders of dogs featured in this book: Stan Brown, Philippe Hardy, Carol Paulsen/La Tutela Kennels, Gonnie Schaffer, K. Shmuely, G. Siano/della Grotta Azzurra and George Small

Large dogs like the Neapolitan Mastiff have been used as guard and war dogs for thousands of years. Julius Caesar met them during the first century BC when he invaded the British Isles.

HISTORY OF THE
NEAPOLITAN MASTIFF

Both the Metropolitan Museum of Art in New York and the Chicago Art Museum house Mesopotamian terracotta artefacts in the likeness of dogs very similar to the modern Neapolitan Mastiff. An extremely large-headed sitting dog with folds of skin, a powerful muzzle and jaws and amputated ears is depicted in the first, and the second shows a female with the same head type and strength, nursing four puppies. An Assyrian terracotta artefact dating back to the 9th century BC resides in a British museum. Master and dog are depicted, with the master holding the dog by his collar. The dog is pictured with natural ears set rather high on the skull, a massive head with many wrinkles, great dewlap reaching from the mouth to mid-neck and a powerfully built rectangular body set on thick legs. The dog's withers reach the master's belt, indicating his massive size.

Let us begin the history with the Sumerians, who bred large and powerful dogs that were used in battle and to hunt lions and other game. The main characteristics of these dogs were their short, strong muzzles, huge and powerful heads, muscular legs, heavy bone and massive body coupled with great height. These dogs must be considered to be the descendants of the ancient Tibetan Mastiff, who authorities say is the forerunner of all molosser-type dogs. As the Sumerians traveled, they brought their dogs to Mesopotamia 2,000 years before the birth of Christ. These mollosers were bred and used to protect property and also to protect livestock from lions. Spreading north, south and east, these dogs eventually reached the Phoenicians. Alexander the Great had many molossians and made a gift of several of these dogs to be taken back to Rome.

During the first century BC, Julius Caesar met with dogs of huge stature and ferocity that he called *Pugnaces Brittaniae* during his campaign in the British Isles. He was so taken with these animals that he took several back to Rome. The presence of these dogs in the British Isles gives credence to the fact that the Phoenicians spread these dogs to the Mediterranean area and points west.

In Roman times the dogs were used as weapons of war and in the circus where they fought wild animals. Handlers and mastiffs fought other handlers and mastiffs in the great coliseums. Roman villas were protected by the mastiffs. After the fall of the Roman Empire, countries were formed and the descendants of these dogs took on the names and the attributes of the countries in which they resided. The dogs that remained in the region near Vesuvius formed a bond with the land and the people. In the days of the Renaissance, the mastiff was used as a hunter of large game and as a guard dog.

Latin author Columella, in the first century AD, wrote in his work *De Re Rustica* about the Roman mastiff that was the guardian of the house at that time, "…because a dark dog has a more terrifying appearance; and during the day, a prowler can see him and be frightened by his appearance. When night falls, the dog, lost in the shadows, can attack without being seen. The head is so massive that it seems to be the most important part of the body. The ears fall toward the front, the brilliant and penetrating eyes are black or gray, the chest is deep and hairy, the shoulder wide, the legs thick, the tail short, the hind legs powerful, the toenails strong and great. His temperament must be neither too gentle nor too ferocious and cruel; whereas the first would make him too apt to welcome a thief, the second would predispose him to attack the people of the house." These words, although written some 2,000 years ago, summarize the current-day Neapolitan Mastiff. Columella goes on to say, "It does not matter that house guard dogs have heavy bodies and are not swift of foot. They are meant to carry out their work from close quarters and do not need to run far." Thus molossians were bred and kept large and

LUPINE ORIGINS

Dogs and wolves are members of the genus *Canis*. Wolves are known scientifically as *Canis lupus* while dogs are known as *Canis domesticus*. Dogs and wolves are known to inter-

breed. The term *canine* derives from the Latin derived word *Canis*. The term *dog* has no scientific basis but has been used for thousands of years. The origin of the word *dog* has never been authoritatively ascertained.

heavy so that they could bring down an animal or a man and not roam from their homes and their duties as guards. It is said that in ancient times masters would cut off their dog's toes and intentionally cripple them for this very same purpose. The Italian molossian remains virtually unchanged from the time of Columella until this day.

The Italian molossian remained hidden in the Italian countryside for centuries, its temperament and uniqueness being preserved. A well-guarded secret, these molossians were bred and kept in the area of Mt. Vesuvius. These relics of a time long gone, with no written word to define the bloodlines, were only brought to light during the latter part of the 1940s. In 1949 Piero Scanziani brought forth this very same dog and it was renamed the Mastino Napoletano. Scanziani, along with other dog enthusiasts, took on the monumental task of writing the standard and ascertaining which of these dogs should be used for breeding. Individuals were visited and measured and their findings recorded. Finally, with written standard in hand, the Mastino Napoletano became a recognized breed with the Italian Kennel Club.

At one point there arose a debate as to the chosen name of our magnificent breed. Some of the breed founders opted for the Molosso Romano as a tribute to the Roman Molossian; others wanted the breed name to be Mastino Napoletano, honoring the people and the area that kept this breed alive for centuries. Mastino Napoletano became the breed name of choice though, in my estimation, I feel that Molosso Romano better describes this dog that survived for so many thousands of years.

Some breeding took place between 1949 and 1960. Breed type was set but was somewhat different from that of today's dogs. Less wrinkled and tighter skinned, the breed began its evolution. The 1970s saw many of the greatest dogs come forth. Dogs like Ital. Ch. Sansone I di Ponzano, Ital. Ch. Leone, Ital. Ch. Socrates di Ponzano, Ital. Ch. Madigam della Grotta Azzurra and Falco della Grotta Azzurra, just to name a few, imprinted their type upon the breed not only in Italy but also in France and other European countries. In the late 1970s, 16 outstanding individuals were imported into Germany where, for some unknown reason, the breeding ceased. These 16 Mastini

The Italian Kennel Club was first to recognize the Neapolitan Mastiff, or Mastino Napoletano.

Neapolitan Mastiff

The Tibetan Mastiff is an Asian guard/war dog. Authorities believe that this breed is the forerunner of all molosser-type dogs.

The Cane Corso is another Italian breed, also part of the mastiff family.

consisted of 10 dogs and 6 bitches. The dogs that were imported from northern Italy were Int. Ch. Enea di Ponzano and Int./Ital. Ch. Aronne. The remaining eight who came from southern Italy were Ital. Ch. Mason della Grotta Azzurra, Attila della Grotta Azzurra, Unno, Sarno, Oro, Ur, Nerone and Ital. Ch. Califf della Dea Partenopea. The bitches Teresina della Casa Lazzarone and Int. Ch. Gilda di Ponzano hailed from the South of Italy while the remaining four—Bundessiegerin Romana della Grotta Azzurra, Europasiegerin Medea della Grotta Azzurra, Valeria della Grotta Azzurra and Europasiegerin Pacchiana—were previously from the North. Very few dogs came out of these excellent specimens; in fact, only Enea was used to any extent in a breeding program. To this day it remains a mystery, although some believe that this mass importation caused a divided camp. Four Germans undertook this importation to improve the breeding of the Mastino in Germany while another small faction did everything in its power to prevent this project from becoming a success, obviously succeeding.

Italian immigrants brought some Neapolitans over to the United States in the early 1900s but the major importer and primary founder of the breed here was Michael Sottile, Sr., president and founder of the NMCA (Neapolitan Mastiff Club of America) in the 1970s. Michael's grandfather, it is said, smuggled four puppies into the United States in

1902. Along with Michael Sr., Jane Pampalone and Joan (Moran) White played important roles in promoting the breed through dog shows and helped the breed gain popularity. In the 1980s breeding stock and puppies were exported from Italy to foreign countries, including the United States. The shores of America saw the offspring of some magnificent dogs such as El Gavilan dell'Altafiumara, Mosé, Squar- cione, Zimbo della Zacchera and Hatrim and Frazier della Grotta Azzurra, just to mention a few.

All of Europe, including Belgium, Hungary, the Nether- lands and the Slavic Republic, saw importation into their home- lands, where excellent dogs are still being produced today. Within the past ten years, a heightened awareness of the breed has arisen in both Australia and England. Long quarantines in these coun-

The Mastiff is one of the more well-known representatives of the breeds whose names include the term *mastiff*.

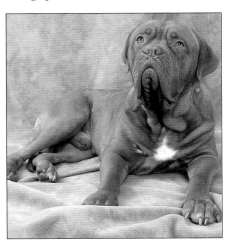

PURE-BRED VIRTUES

Since dogs have been inbred for centuries, their physical and mental characteristics are constantly being changed to suit man's desires for hunting, retrieving, scenting, guarding and warming their master's laps. During the past 150 years, dogs have been judged according to physical characteristics as well as functional abilities. Few breeds can boast a genuine balance between physique, working ability and temperament.

The Dogue de Bordeaux is a rare mastiff breed that is becoming quite popular, especially in southern Europe.

13

Neapolitan Mastiff

An adult Neo with natural ears; the puppy's ears have been cropped.

Vera della Grotta Azzurra at two months of age. She is a blue bitch owned by La Tutela Kennels.

tries has made it quite cost-prohibitive to import puppies and older breeding stock, but there are determined breeders making their mark.

The Neapolitan is experiencing great popularity in the United States at the present time and we are finding more dogs needing rehoming from shelters and unsuitable homes. This is the price a breed pays for notoriety.

Mastinari is the Italian word used for the true Neapolitan Mastiff breeder, a connoisseur and a true artist of the breed, whose blood, sweat and tears have culminated in breeding and producing Mastini that can be considered magnificent creations. This term is not applied to any newcomer to the breed nor ever applied "lightly" to just any individual breeder. The ideal Neapolitan Mastiff is the true *Mastinari*'s mission and goal. We must pay homage to them for preserving our ancient and noble breed.

15

NEAPOLITAN MASTIFF

PHYSICAL CHARACTERISTICS
The following excerpt is taken from the 1971 Fédération Cynologique Internationale (FCI) standard for the Neapolitan Mastiff describing the general appearance, conformation, balance and disposition: "The Neapolitan Mastiff is a guard dog and defense dog par excellence, of great size, powerful and strongly built, of tough yet majestic appearance, sturdy and courageous, of intelligent expression, endowed with correct mental balance and docile character, non-aggressive, indefatigable defender of persons and property. The general conformation is that of a heavy brachymorph, whose trunk is longer than the height at the withers, harmonious as regards size (heterometry) and profile (alloidism). Skin is not adhering to the underlying tissue but abundant, with slack connective tissue over all parts of the body and especially on the head where it forms wrinkles and folds and at the neck where it forms the dewlap." A better description of this majestic beast can never be found.

Massive is a word which best describes the Neapolitan Mastiff. A large and powerful dog with a brachycephalic and massive skull, wrinkled head, huge bone and stocky body, the typical Neapolitan male weighs in at 150 lbs. and stands 29 in. at the withers. Females are somewhat smaller in size, typically 130 lbs. The Neapolitan is certainly not the tallest of dogs but next to his English Mastiff cousin, the Neapolitan more often than not appears to be more broad and massive though lighter. Adult height is usually reached at about one year of age, though some

Why are people drawn to the Neapolitan Mastiff? The breed's unique look, guarding ability and even temperament are several of the many reasons.

Neos take a long time to mature, often not reaching their adult weight until over three years of age.

individuals may grow an inch or so more after that. Adult weight is generally not reached until the dog is three to three-and-a-half years of age and sometimes older. Like all giant breeds, the Neapolitan is slow to mature and his puppyhood is long. He is not considered to be a mature specimen until the age of three. Unfortunately, this wonderful animal, like all other giant breeds, does not have a long life. The Neapolitan's lifespan is eight to ten years.

Having a short, stiff, hard and dense coat of uniform length and smoothness all over the body, the Neapolitan Mastiff is virtually a wash-and-wear dog. No extensive grooming is required except during the two shedding periods, spring and fall. I find that a shedding blade coupled with a mitt of sisal or horsehair will help remove all dead hair. The accepted coat colors are black, blue (all shades of gray), tawny and mahogany, all with or without brindling (a slight striping on all or part of the coat). Brindling is not a color but a marking. White markings are acceptable on tips of toes and on the chest. All puppies are born with blue eyes that change to correspond to the coat color at three to four months of age. In black dogs the eyes are

17

usually brown; hazel is common in the blue specimens. The natural ear of the Neapolitan is small in relation to the size of the dog. It is triangular in shape, set above the zygomatic arch (cheekbone) and lying flat and close to the cheek. Traditionally cropped, they form an equilateral triangle.

Cropping of the ear is not required for the show ring; Neapolitans may be shown with natural ears or cropped ears. The cropped ear gives the dog a more alert expression. The tail is always docked to two-thirds of its original length, reaching or slightly exceeding the top of the hock. The tail should be

Neos are born with drop ears, yet many owners choose to have their dogs' ears cropped to give a more alert expression.

broad and thick at the root, tapering slightly at the tip and set slightly lower than the dog's topline.

PERSONALITY

The Neapolitan Mastiff is a loyal, peaceful and steady dog, not aggressive or prone to biting without reason. A superior guardian of his persons and property, the Neapolitan is a vigilant, intelligent, noble and majestic beast. It is not uncommon for the Neapolitan to be stubborn, headstrong, independent and strong-willed, and sometimes shy; however, shy dogs should never be bred. Wary of strangers but a wonderful, loving companion with his own family, the Neapolitan needs socialization to become accustomed to different people, places and things. Most Neapolitans prefer to be homebodies and are not advocates of change. Social interaction with people is a must and the Neapolitan should be taken off the premises, touched and petted by as many people as possible when still a puppy. When the interaction is positive, the Neapolitan should be showered with praise. Most owners are concerned that high levels of socialization will diminish the Neapolitan's ability to be a guard dog and protect his home and family, but nothing could be further from the truth. This trait has been bred into the breed for

The female Neo, shown here, is typically smaller than the male, weighing on average about 20 lbs. less.

centuries; it is not changed that easily. It is imperative, though, that an owner of a Neapolitan never forget the dog's strong, natural and primitive instincts. The Neapolitan Mastiff owner, in order to raise a good canine citizen, must always be aware of the thoughts and behavior of dogs, and must couple this awareness with responsible, consistent discipline.

Because of the love the Neapolitan has for his home and family, he will not stray—a wanderer he is not. His master is everything to the Neapolitan; he would rather be with his master than do anything else. He seeks the companionship of his master more so than that of another dog or animal. Your Neapolitan will follow you from room to room and lie at your feet waiting for your next move. His master is his world. This being said, it is no surprise that the Neapolitan Mastiff is loyal to a fault. A few kind words and loving touches will endear you to him forever.

Neapolitans by nature are dominant alpha dogs and must be handled accordingly. It is important to remember that every member of the family, including the children, must outrank the Neapolitan in pack member status. Please be aware that the Neapolitan is an adult's dog, not a dog meant for children's entertain-ment. If you are looking for a dog for your children to be their nursemaid and to play with, then consider another breed. As a rule, no dog, large or small, should be left with children unattended. This is an accident waiting to happen; if you are unable to supervise your dog around chil-dren, please separate the dog from them. All activity, including play, between the Neapolitan and the children should be done in the presence of at least one adult. Most Neapolitans are fond of their human children and would not purposely hurt them, but, because

The Neapolitan Mastiff is a dog for adults; they must never be left alone with children. While most Neos would not intentionally hurt anyone, their large size can be dangerous to small children.

of their large size, they could knock over a small child and step on him in their exuberance. The Neapolitan deserves and commands respect from adults and children alike.

Neapolitans are generally tolerant of other animals but it is not recommended that the Neapolitan share the household with another dog with an alpha nature. If two Neapolitans of the same sex are housed together, they may have to be separated as the severity of their disagreements increases. When a female is kept with a male Neapolitan, she usually takes charge if the male allows himself to become

The Neo is a giant dog. This is not a breed to be carried around; as they grow, it doesn't take long before they become too heavy to lift.

DOGS, DOGS, GOOD FOR YOUR HEART!

People usually purchase dogs for companionship, but studies show that dogs can help to improve their owners' health and level of activity, as well as lower a human's risk of coronary heart disease. Without even realising it, when a person puts time into exercising, grooming and feeding a dog, he also puts more time into his own personal health care. Dog owners establish a more routine schedule for their dogs to follow, which can have positive effects on a human's health. Dogs also teach us patience, offer unconditional love and provide the joy of having a furry friend to pet!

subservient. I have seen males and females fight for the alpha position in the pack. I recommend, from my own personal experiences, that each dog, male and female, be housed separately when left alone to prevent fighting and bloodshed. It truly is not worthwhile having your prized possession maimed or disfigured because you are seeking the "Peaceable Kingdom."

Loving the chase, the Neapolitan will often pursue a runner or bicyclist, and most have been known to chase cats and other quick-moving animals like rabbits. This is why it is important that the Neapolitan be obedience trained and his energy channeled properly. All dogs must be taught

21

Neapolitan Mastiff

You really have to love the breed if you want to own a Neo. Such a large dog requires a lot of room and a lot of food, not to mention the unique grooming requirements of a loose-skinned breed.

mended that crate training be employed.

It should be noted that the Neapolitan is the messiest of eaters. His copious flews and large lips scatter food in all directions and are great hiding places for snacks long after the meal is over. Neapolitans need significant quantities of both food and water, and with drinking and eating comes the drool. All Neapolitans drool to some extent. Their drool is a heavy, thick saliva with the consistency of egg whites. Most Neapolitans do not drool all the time, although I have had some, three males in particular come to mind, that seemed as if their mouths were perpetual faucets. Drooling can and does also occur during periods of nervousness and hot weather conditions.

Another endearing habit of the Neapolitan, as is true with all mastiff-type dogs, is snoring. A sound-asleep Neapolitan resting contentedly on the second floor of a house can be heard on the first floor right through the floor-boards! This certainly does not sit well with humans who tend to be light sleepers.

The Neapolitan is not a suitable dog for everyone. It is definitely not for the first-time dog owner, and the prospective owner should have some experience with dominant alpha dogs. The Neapolitan cannot be expected to spend his entire life isolated in a

what is acceptable and unacceptable behavior; therefore, obedience training for the Neapolitan is a must. Consistency is the key. With a dog the size of the Neapolitan, it is imperative that the owner be in charge at all times. The owner has this obligation to himself, to his dog and to others.

Neapolitans love to chew; adequate toys and various types of bones should help to alleviate this problem. However, until he can be safely left in the home without causing destruction, it is recom-

22

backyard with only food and water and no attention or socialization. Neapolitans need attention, discipline and human companionship. A Neapolitan is a large, vocal and messy animal, so in all fairness to the dog, please research the breed carefully.

WORKING DOG OR HOME COMPANION?

The Neapolitan Mastiff is a natural guard. To try to separate the companion dog from the working dog in this breed is an impossible task. They are always on guard—this is their job—and they will do it while being your companion. The Neapolitan takes his job as a working dog seriously. His fierce appearance and gargoyle-like head add to his being a deterrent to home intrusion. Although appearing slow and lumbering, the Neapolitan can become aroused in a moment to protect his property or his charges. However, on the whole, the Neapolitan is an even-tempered animal who loves to cuddle up on the couch and sleep, reserving his energy for times when it is needed. He is not a patroling dog by nature; he watches and waits and strikes when necessary.

Neapolitan Mastiffs are not particularly active or fast-moving dogs. Their large, heavy size prevents them from moving too quickly.

VERSATILITY AND AGILITY

The role of the Neapolitan is that of a guardian. This is what he was bred for and he does his job well. We have since broadened the horizons for this majestic breed opening up new and different challenges for our Mastini. In obedience work Neapolitans seem to do well in a class setting, but in formal obedience trials they are not the quick-responding dog that the Shepherds, Aussies, Goldens or Shelties are. They are generally slow moving and contemplative, almost mulling over the commands before acting on them. Obedience judges are just starting to recognize this, and more mastiff dogs are receiving higher obedience scores.

The Neapolitan is not the best selection of a dog for athletic ability and endurance. Yes, there are some that excel, but they are the exceptions. Running along-side a bike and jogging are not the Neapolitan's forte. They are heavy for their height and their stamina is not the greatest; they fatigue and overheat easily. Most Neapolitan Mastiffs love to swim and this is a good form of exer-cise for them since it is gentle on their joints and limbs. Puppies should never be heavily exer-cised, as this will result in damage to the joints and liga-ments that will cause skeletal damage as they grow. Short walks for a small puppy are fine and stair climbing should be limited. The Neapolitan has a very high tolerance for pain and, because of this, injuries can go unnoticed and untreated.

HEALTH CONSIDERATIONS AND HEREDITARY DISEASES
One of the unique features of the Neapolitan is his loose skin and wrinkles. Despite what one would think from his appearance, the Neapolitan generally does not suffer from skin problems. The dog should be kept clean and parasite-free and there should be no skin problems.

Demodicosis (demodectic mange) generally runs in certain lines, and dogs suffering from weak immune systems displaying this disease should be spayed or neutered and not bred. The mites, which inhabit all dogs, multiply in such abundant numbers that they cause hair to fall out, pustules to form and infection to set in. This is usually seen in puppies but it has been known to appear in females during estrus and some males reaching puberty. Your veterinarian can recommend

the appropriate topical solution and/or oral antibiotics for the irritation.

Emotionally and economically, the *Demodex* mite reeks havoc on both the Neapolitan Mastiff and his owner, but once treatment is complete all is back to normal. Be aware that this condition is hereditary and that breeding animals that have been prone to *Demodex* and that have poor immune systems can and do add to the canine population's suffering from skin disorders.

Cherry eye is a problem in the Neapolitan but is not unique to this breed. It is simply the prolapse of the gland of the third eyelid. The loose connective tissue of the Neapolitan contributes to this ailment. This unsightly red and swollen gland can be removed under anesthesia by snipping it out. Some veterinarians advocate tacking the gland back down under the third eyelid, but this procedure has never been seen to work successfully in the Neapolitan. Contrary to popular belief, removal of the gland, if done correctly, will not cause "dry eye" or reoccurrence. The third eyelid must be left intact.

Canine hip dysplasia and elbow dysplasia are also seen in the Neapolitan Mastiff. Complex in nature, these two conditions are fairly common in large and small breeds alike. The Neapolitan has loose joints and connective tissue, but joint laxity does not equate to hip dysplasia. At present, there are many prescription medications and over-the-counter medications to alleviate the symptoms of hip dysplasia. There are also various surgical procedures to correct the problem. These options should be discussed with your veterinarian on a case-by-case basis. Suffice it to say that only sound, beautiful specimens should be bred.

Ruptured anterior cruciate liga-

The Neapolitan Mastiff is constantly on guard; it is his job by instinct. Having this Neo watching over your property means that your home is well protected.

25

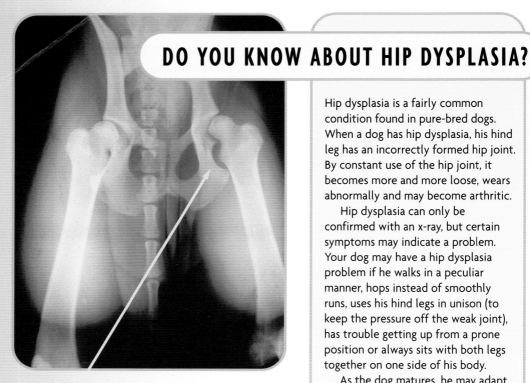

DO YOU KNOW ABOUT HIP DYSPLASIA?

Hip dysplasia is a fairly common condition found in pure-bred dogs. When a dog has hip dysplasia, his hind leg has an incorrectly formed hip joint. By constant use of the hip joint, it becomes more and more loose, wears abnormally and may become arthritic.

Hip dysplasia can only be confirmed with an x-ray, but certain symptoms may indicate a problem. Your dog may have a hip dysplasia problem if he walks in a peculiar manner, hops instead of smoothly runs, uses his hind legs in unison (to keep the pressure off the weak joint), has trouble getting up from a prone position or always sits with both legs together on one side of his body.

As the dog matures, he may adapt well to life with a bad hip, but in a few years the arthritis develops and many dogs with hip dysplasia become crippled.

Hip dysplasia is considered an inherited disease and can only be diagnosed definitely when the dog is two years old. Some experts claim that a special diet might help your puppy outgrow the bad hip, but the usual treatments are surgical. The removal of the pectineus muscle, the removal of the round part of the femur, reconstructing the pelvis and replacing the hip with an artificial one are all surgical interventions that are expensive, but they are usually very successful. Follow the advice of your veterinarian.

Hip dysplasia is a badly worn hip joint caused by improper fit of the bone into the socket. It is easily the most common hip problem in larger dogs. The illustration shows a healthy hip joint on the left and an unhealthy hip joint on the right.

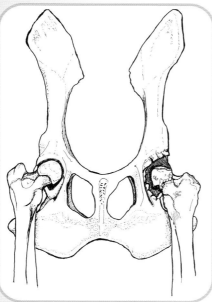

ment, "football injury," occurs when the dog suffers trauma to the stifle. This can happen while running and turning improperly on the back legs, tearing the ligament that holds the knee together. A competent orthopedic surgeon should be sought out for the surgery. Rest and no stair climbing are recommended after the procedure.

Panosteitis (or wandering lameness or growing pains) usually appears in puppies 4 to 18 months of age and usually subsides as the dog reaches the age of two. Symptoms are limping, pain traveling from leg to leg and difficulty in jumping and getting up. Rest is the treatment recommended along with some anti-inflammatory medications.

Entropion (turning in of the eyelid) and ectropion (turning out of the eyelid) are seen in some specimens. This too can be surgically corrected if it is not outgrown in puppies.

The Neapolitan tolerates cold weather better than he does the heat. Thus, it is quite easy for a Neapolitan to suffer overheating and stroke. Water and shade should always be made available to outside dogs. Hosing them down will help to keep them cool during hot summer weather. Many a Neapolitan has died because his owner did not provide proper conditions for his survival in hot and humid temperatures. Even though short-haired, the Neapolitan can easily tolerate freezing, even below-freezing, winter weather as long as he has shelter from the cold and the elements. Bedding can, and should, consist of straw, as straw provides warmth and comfort and is not easily broken down.

Another issue of concern in the Neapolitan Mastiff is the breed's low tolerance for anesthesia and tranquilizers. Many a Neapolitan has died on the operating table because of an overdose of anesthesia. The veterinarian should be made aware of this prior to surgery. Tranquilizers also should be given with a light hand. Dosage can always be increased, but once ingested it can be difficult and nearly impossible to reverse.

Large breeds are prone to the crippling condition known as hip dysplasia. This is a condition of the hip joints, in which the bones do not fit into the hip sockets properly.

BREED STANDARD FOR THE
NEAPOLITAN MASTIFF

The Neapolitan Mastiff gained American Kennel Club recognition in 2004 and currently competes in the Working Group at AKC shows. The Neapolitan Mastiff is also recognized by the Fédération Cynologique Internationale (FCI), the main registry body in Europe, as well as by the Italian Kennel Club (ENCI), the Australian National Kennel Council and the Canadian Kennel Club.

A breed standard, which is the written description of the ideal representative of a breed, is used by breeders and judges to assess the quality of dogs in a breeding program and the show ring. Here we present the official AKC breed standard that was approved in January 2004.

AMERICAN KENNEL CLUB STANDARD FOR THE NEAPOLITAN MASTIFF
General Appearance: An ancient breed, rediscovered in Italy in the 1940s, the Neapolitan Mastiff is a heavy-boned, massive, awe inspiring dog bred for use as a guard and defender of owner and

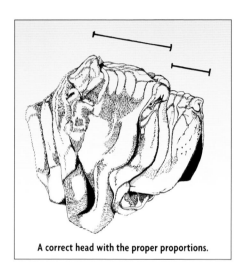

A correct head with the proper proportions.

property. He is characterized by loose skin, over his entire body, abundant, hanging wrinkles and folds on the head and a voluminous dewlap. The essence of the Neapolitan is his bestial appearance, astounding head and imposing size and attitude. Due to his massive structure, his characteristic movement is rolling and lumbering, not elegant or showy.

Size, Proportion, Substance
A stocky, heavy boned dog, massive in substance, rectangular

in proportion. Length of body is 10% to 15% greater than height. *Height:* Dogs: 26 to 31 inches, Bitches: 24 to 29 inches. Average weight of mature dogs: 150

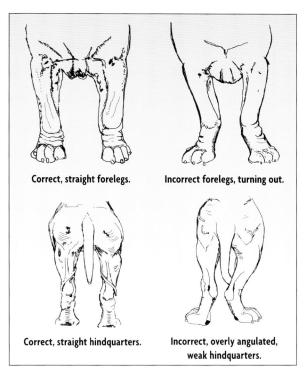

Correct, straight forelegs.

Incorrect forelegs, turning out.

Correct, straight hindquarters.

Incorrect, overly angulated, weak hindquarters.

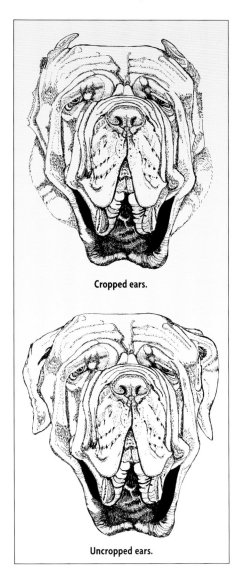

Cropped ears.

Uncropped ears.

pounds; bitches: 110 pounds; but greater weight is usual and preferable as long as correct proportion and function are maintained. The absence of massiveness is to be so severely penalized as to eliminate from competition.

Head: Large in comparison to the body. Differentiated from that of other mastiff breeds by more extensive wrinkling and pendulous lips which blend into an ample dewlap. Toplines of cranium and the muzzle must be parallel. The face is made up of heavy wrinkles and folds.

Neapolitan Mastiff

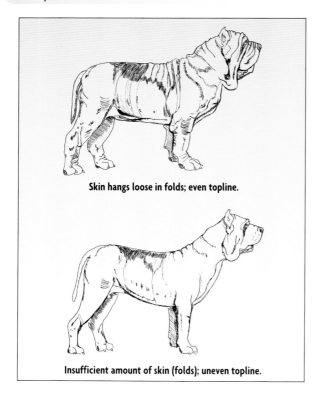

Skin hangs loose in folds; even topline.

Insufficient amount of skin (folds); uneven topline.

Required folds are those extending from the outside margin of the eyelids to the dewlap, and from under the lower lids to the outer edges of the lips. *Severe Faults:* Toplines of the cranium and muzzle not parallel. *Disqualification*: Absence of wrinkles and folds. *Expression:* Wistful at rest, intimidating when alert. Penetrating stare. *Eyes:* Set deep and almost hidden beneath drooping upper lids. Lower lids droop to reveal haw. *Eye Color:* Shades of amber or brown, in accordance with coat color.

Pigmentation of the eye rims same as coat color. *Severe Faults:* Whitish-blue eyes; incomplete pigmentation of the eye rims. *Ears:* Set well above the cheekbones. May be cropped or uncropped, but are usually cropped to an equilateral triangle for health reasons. If uncropped, they are medium sized, triangular in shape, held tight to the cheeks, and not extending beyond the lower margin of the throat. *Skull:* Wide flat between the ears, slightly arched at the frontal part, and covered with wrinkled skin. The width of the cranium between the cheekbones is approximately equal to its length from occiput stop. The brow is very developed. Frontal furrow is marked. Occiput is barely apparent. *Stop:* Very defined, forming a right angle at the junction of muzzle and frontal bones, and the sloping back at a greater angle where the frontal bones meet the frontal furrow of the forehead. *Nose:* Large with well-opened nostrils, and in color the same as the coat. The nose is an extension of the topline of the muzzle and should not protrude beyond nor recede behind the front plane of the muzzle. *Severe Fault*: Incomplete pigmentation of the nose. *Muzzle:* It is one-third the length of the whole head and is as broad as it is long. Viewed from the front, the muzzle is very deep with the outside borders parallel giving it a "squared" appearance. The top plane of the muzzle from stop to tip of nose is straight, but is ridged due to heavy folds of skin covering it. *Severe Faults:* Top plane of the muzzle curved upward or downward. *Lips:* Heavy, thick, and long, the upper lips join beneath the nostrils to form an inverted "V." The upper lips form the lower, outer borders of the muzzle, and the lowest part of these borders is made by the corners of the lips. The corners turn outward to reveal the flews, and are in line with the outside corners of the eyes. *Bite:* Scissors bite or pincer bite is standard; slight undershot is allowed. Dentition is complete. *Faults:* More than 1 missing premolar. *Severe Faults:* Overshot jaw; pronounced undershot jaw which disrupts the outline of the front plane of the muzzle; more than 2 missing teeth.

Neck, Topline and Body
Neck: Slightly arched, rather short, stocky and well-muscled. The voluminous and well-divided dewlap extends from the lower jaw to the lower neck. *Disqualification:* Absence of dewlap. *Body:* The length of the dog, measured from the point of the shoulder to the point of buttock is 10 to 15 percent greater than the height of the dog measured from the highest point of the shoulder to

When a Neo has a sufficient amount of skin, his facial wrinkles can be extended as shown.

the ground. Depth of the ribcage is equal to half the total height of the dog. Ribs are long and well sprung. *Chest:* Broad and deep, well muscled. *Underline and Tuckup:* The underline of the abdomen is practically horizontal. There is little or no tuckup. *Back:* Wide and strong. Highest part of shoulder blade barely rising above the strong, level topline of the back. *Loin:* Well-muscled, and harmoniously joined to the back. *Croup:* Wide, strong, muscular and slightly sloped. The top of the croup rises slightly and is level with the highest point of the shoulder. *Tail:* Set on slightly lower than the topline, wide and thick at the root, tapering gradually toward the tip. It is docked by one-third. At rest, the tail hangs straight or in slight "S" shape. When in action, it is raised to the horizontal or a little higher than the back. *Severe Faults:* Tail carried straight up or curved over the back. Kinked tail. *Disqualifications:* Lack of tail or short tail,

31

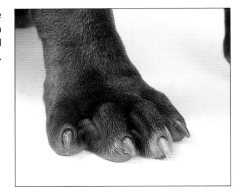

Close-up of the Neo's foot, with nicely trimmed nails.

Hindquarters: As a whole, they must be powerful and strong, in harmony with the forequarters. *Thighs:* About the same length as the forearms, broad, muscular. *Stifles:* Moderate angle, strong. *Legs:* Heavy and thick boned, well-muscled. Slightly shorter than thigh bones. *Hocks:* Powerful and long. *Rear Pasterns:* (metatarsus) Heavy thick bones. Viewed from the side, they are perpendicular to the ground. Viewed from the rear, parallel to each other. *Rear Dewclaws:* Any dewclaws must be removed. *Hind Feet:* Same as the front feet but slightly smaller.

which is less than one-third the length from point of insertion of the tail to the hock-joint.

Forequarters: Heavily built, muscular, and in balance with the hindquarters. *Shoulders:* Long, well-muscled, sloping and powerful. Upper arms: Strongly muscled, powerful. In length, almost one-third the height of the dog. *Elbows:* Covered with abundant and loose skin; held parallel to the ribcage, neither tied in nor loose. *Forelegs:* Thick, straight, heavy bone, well muscled, exemplifying strength. About the same length as the upper arms. Set well apart. *Pasterns:* Thick and flattened from front to back, moderately sloping forward from the leg. *Dewclaws:* Front dewclaws are not removed. *Feet:* Round and noticeably large with arched, strong toes. Nails strong, curved and preferably dark-colored. Slight turn out of the front feet is characteristic.

The Neo's chest should be broad and wide with elbows not held too closely.

Coat: The coat is short, dense and of uniform length and smoothness all over the body. The hairs are straight and not longer than 1 inch. No fringe anywhere.

Color: Solid coats of gray (blue), black, mahogany and tawny, and the lighter and darker shades of these colors. Some brindling allowable in all colors. When present, brindling must be tan (reverse brindle). There may be solid white markings on the chest, throat area from chin to chest, underside of the body, penis sheath, backs of the pasterns, and on the toes. There may be white hairs at the back of the wrists. *Disqualification:* White markings on any part of the body not mentioned as allowed.

Gait: The Neapolitan Mastiff's movement is not flashy, but rather slow and lumbering. Normal gaits are the walk, trot, gallop, and pace. The strides are long and elastic, at the same time, powerful, characterized by a long push from the hindquarters and extension of the forelegs. Rolling motion and swaying of the body at all gaits is characteristic. Pacing in the show ring is not to be penalized. Slight paddling movement of the front feet is normal. The head is carried level with or slightly above the back.

Temperament: The Neapolitan Mastiff is steady and loyal to his owner, not aggressive or apt to bite without reason. As a protector of his property and owners, he is always watchful and does not relish intrusion by strangers into his personal space. His attitude is calm yet wary. In the show ring he is majestic and powerful, but not showy.

Faults: The foregoing description is that of the ideal Neapolitan Mastiff. Any deviation from the above described dog must be penalized to the extent of the deviation.

Disqualifications: Absence of wrinkles and folds; absence of dewlap; lack of tail or short tail, which is less than one-third the length from point of insertion of the tail to the hock; white markings on any part of the body not mentioned.

Effective May 1, 2004

A very nicely proportioned Neapolitan Mastiff in an alert pose.

YOUR PUPPY

NEAPOLITAN MASTIFF

Purchase a puppy from a responsible, experienced breeder who cares about each puppy he places and the whole breed itself.

Selecting a pure-bred dog from a responsible breeder will allow for a higher degree of predictability regarding temperament, health, working ability, size, coat, etc. A responsible breeder cares about each dog he brings into the world and will take positive steps to ensure that his dogs do not land in a shelter or rescue. Responsible breeders require deposits before puppies are born to encourage commitment from potential owners. They interview the interested parties and are honest about

ARE YOU PREPARED?

Unfortunately, when a puppy is bought by someone who does not take into consideration the time and attention that dog ownership requires, it is the puppy who suffers when he is either abandoned or placed in a shelter by a frustrated owner. So all of the "homework" you do in preparation for your pup's arrival will benefit you both. The more informed you are, the more you will know what to expect and the better equipped you will be to handle the ups and downs of raising a puppy. Hopefully, everyone in the household is willing to do his part in raising and caring for the pup. The anticipation of owning a dog often brings a lot of promises from excited family members: "I will walk him every day," "I will feed him," "I will house-train him," etc., but these things take time and effort, and promises can easily be forgotten once the novelty of the new pet has worn off.

A HEALTHY PUP

You should not even think about buying a puppy that looks sick, undernourished, overly frightened or nervous. Sometimes a timid puppy will warm up to you after a 30-minute "let's-get-acquainted" session.

the qualities of the dogs they have bred. They will always be available to their buyers to answer questions regarding raising, training and caring for the new puppy. A responsible breeder will always take back or help place a dog they have bred.

Responsible breeders know the typical genetic diseases of the breed and do not breed dogs that may pass on genetic problems. They ensure that the dogs they produce are capable of full, healthy, happy lives, sound in mind, body and temperament. Shy and aggressive dogs are never a good choice for a pet owner.

A responsible breeder is usually active in dog clubs and shows his dogs. Litters are kept to a minimum, usually one to three per year. Responsible breeders are in touch with their puppy buyers, even after a period of years. The breeder should be curious about you, concerned about the welfare of his puppies. The breeder will ask you questions and insist on certain criteria being met before

placing a puppy. A good responsible breeder will be willing to discuss all the genetic problems, nutrition, socialization and training of your puppy with you. He should be there for you for the remainder of your puppy's life.

Where possible, the kennel should be visited. The kennel usually consists of indoor/outdoor runs and exercise yards, or it may be simply the breeder's home. It should be clean and free of excre-

ment, just like the puppies. This goes for all of the dogs in the kennel—they should all be clean and brushed and should have fresh food and water. The runs should be large enough to accommodate the size of the dog contained therein. The dogs should appear healthy, friendly and outgoing towards humans; the health of the older dogs on the premises will tell you a great deal about the kennel.

Human contact is important, so the first few weeks of a puppy's life

The time you spend getting to know your new puppy will form a bond that lasts a lifetime.

35

be active and playful, eager to meet people and not shy. There should be no discharge from the eyes, nose or ears, and the gums should be pink and firm. A puppy should be plump, but without a distended belly, and should move around freely without signs of lameness. Pick a puppy that will naturally follow you, is not upset over sudden, loud sounds and has confidence to explore new areas without fear.

Your puppy should have had at least one set of shots, preferably two, and should have been dewormed and examined by a veterinarian. Your breeder of choice should provide you with a pedigree, registration papers, test results, pamphlets on puppy care, feeding instructions and maintenance and a written guarantee covering genetic and congenital problems at the time of puppy purchase. Most of all, trust your common sense and your instincts—if it does not feel right, walk away.

The ideal situation when purchasing a puppy is the ability to see both sire and dam but, when this is not possible, at least the dam should be available for viewing. The dam should be in good condition—healthy, strong, well-fed and possessing the proper look and temperament that would warrant her being bred. The puppies should be available for viewing at eight weeks of age

A new puppy means potty accidents around your home until he is house-broken. Be prepared.

should be shared with humans to form the proper bond. Puppies should always be raised in the house in constant contact with people, sounds and everyday household events. Puppies should

TEMPERAMENT COUNTS

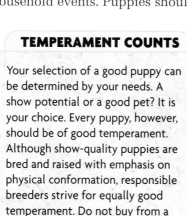

Your selection of a good puppy can be determined by your needs. A show potential or a good pet? It is your choice. Every puppy, however, should be of good temperament. Although show-quality puppies are bred and raised with emphasis on physical conformation, responsible breeders strive for equally good temperament. Do not buy from a breeder who concentrates solely on physical beauty at the expense of personality.

Puppies get a healthy start in life from their dam's milk. A nursing dam is very easy to spot!

when the immunity provided from their dam's milk has worn off and their vaccinations have taken hold. Once the puppy goes home with a new owner, the veterinarian will continue the pup on an appropriate vaccination schedule.

COMMITMENT OF OWNERSHIP

After considering all of these factors, you have most likely already made some very important decisions about selecting

PUPPY APPEARANCE

Your puppy should have a well-fed appearance but not a distended abdomen, which may indicate worms or incorrect feeding, or both. The body should be firm, with a solid feel. The skin of the abdomen should be pale pink and clean, without signs of scratching or rash. Check the hind legs to make certain that dewclaws were removed, if any were present at birth.

37

Neapolitan Mastiff

your puppy. You have chosen a Neapolitan Mastiff, which means that you have decided which characteristics you want in a dog and what type of dog will best fit into your family and lifestyle. If you have selected a breeder, you have gone a step further—you have done your research and found a responsible, conscientious person who breeds quality Neapolitan Mastiffs and who

PEDIGREE VS. REGISTRATION CERTIFICATE

Too often new owners are confused between these two important documents. Your puppy's pedigree, essentially a family tree, is a written record of a dog's genealogy of three generations or more. The pedigree will show you the names as well as performance titles of all the dogs in your pup's background. Your breeder must provide you with a registration application, with his part properly filled out. You must complete the application and send it to your chosen dog registry with the proper fee. The seller must provide you with complete records to identify the puppy. The seller should provide the buyer with the following: breed; sex; color and markings; date of birth; litter number (when available); names and registration numbers of the parents; breeder's name; and date sold or delivered.

should be a reliable source of help as you and your puppy adjust to life together. If you have observed a litter in action, you have obtained a firsthand look at the dynamics of a puppy "pack" and, thus, you should learn about each pup's individual personality—perhaps you have even found one that particularly appeals to you.

However, even if you have not yet found the Neapolitan Mastiff puppy of your dreams, observing pups will help you learn to recognize certain behavior and to determine what a pup's behavior indicates about his temperament. You will be able to pick out which pups are the leaders, which ones are less outgoing, which ones are confident, which ones are shy, playful, friendly, aggressive, etc. Equally

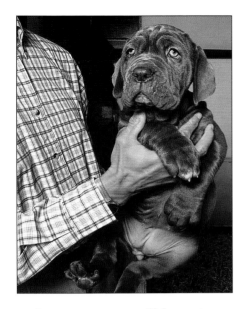

is one instance in which you actually do get to choose your own family! You may be thinking that buying a puppy should be fun—it should not be so serious and so much work. Keep in mind that your puppy is not a cuddly stuffed toy or decorative lawn ornament, but a creature that will become a real member of your family. You will come to realize that, while buying a puppy is a pleasurable and exciting endeavor, it is not something to be taken lightly. Relax...the fun will start when the pup comes home!

The puppy you choose should be healthy and friendly. He should not shy away from being petted and handled.

as important, you will learn to recognize what a healthy pup should look and act like. All of these things will help you in your search, and when you find the Neapolitan Mastiff that was meant for you, you will know it!

Researching your breed, selecting a responsible breeder and observing as many pups as possible are all important steps on the way to dog ownership. It may seem like a lot of effort...and you have not even brought the pup home yet! Remember, though, you cannot be too careful when it comes to deciding on the type of dog you want and finding out about your prospective pup's background. Buying a puppy is not—or should not be—just another whimsical purchase. This

PET INSURANCE

Just as you can insure your car, your house and your own health, you likewise can insure your dog's health. Investigate a pet insurance policy by talking to your vet. Depending on the age of your dog, the breed and the kind of coverage you desire, your policy can be very affordable. Most policies cover accidental injuries, poisoning, and thousands of medical problems and illnesses, including cancers. Some carriers also offer routine care and immunization coverage, including heartworm preventative, prescription flea control, annual checkups, teeth cleaning, spaying/neutering, health screening and more. These policies are more costly than the others, but may be well worth the investment.

39

Always keep in mind that a puppy is nothing more than a baby in a furry disguise…a baby who is virtually helpless in a human world and who trusts his owner for fulfillment of his basic needs for survival. In addition to food, water and shelter, your pup needs care, protection, guidance and love. If you are not prepared to commit to this, then you are not prepared to own a dog.

"Wait a minute", you say. "How hard could this be? All of my neighbors own dogs and they seem to be doing just fine. Why should I have to worry about all of this?" Well, you should not worry about it; in fact, you will probably find that once your Neapolitan Mastiff pup gets used to his new home, he will fall into his place in the family quite naturally. But it never hurts to emphasize the commitment of dog ownership. With some time and patience, it is really not too difficult to raise a curious and active Neapolitan Mastiff pup to be a well-adjusted and well-mannered adult dog—a dog that could be your most loyal friend.

PREPARING PUPPY'S PLACE

Researching your breed and finding a breeder are only two aspects of the "homework" you will have to do before bringing your Neapolitan Mastiff puppy home. You will also have to prepare your home and family for the new addition. Much as you would prepare a nursery for a newborn baby, you will need to designate a place in your home that will be the puppy's own. How you prepare your home will depend on how much freedom the dog will be allowed. Whatever you decide, you must ensure that he has a place that he can "call his own."

When you bring your new puppy into your home, you are bringing him into what will become his home as well. Obviously, you did not buy a puppy so that he could take over your house, but in order for a puppy to grow into a stable, well-adjusted dog, he has to feel comfortable in his surroundings. Remember, he is leaving the warmth and security of his mother and littermates, as well as the familiarity of the only place he has ever known, so it is important to make his transition as easy as possible. By preparing a place in your home for the puppy, you are making him feel as welcome as possible in a strange new place. It should not take him long to get used to it, but the sudden shock of being transplanted is somewhat traumatic for a young pup. Imagine how a small child would feel in the same situation—that is how your puppy must be feeling. It is up to you to reassure him and to let him know, "Little fellow, you are going to like it here!"

ARE YOU A FIT OWNER?

If the breeder from whom you are buying a puppy asks you a lot of personal questions, do not be insulted. Such a breeder wants to be sure that you will be a fit provider for his puppy.

puppies as well as show puppies. Provided the crate is used sparingly, it can be effective for the Neo. Crate training is a very popular and very successful

WHAT YOU SHOULD BUY

CRATE

To someone unfamiliar with the use of crates in dog training, it may seem like punishment to shut a dog in a crate, but this is not the case at all. Although all breeders do not advocate crate training, many breeders and trainers are recommending crates as a preferred tool for pet

housebreaking method. A crate can keep your dog safe during travel; and, perhaps most importantly, a crate provides your dog with a place of his own in your home. It serves as a "doggie bedroom" of sorts—your Neapolitan Mastiff can curl up in his crate when he wants to sleep or when he just needs a break. Many dogs sleep in their crates overnight. When lined with soft

A litter of baby Neos, each one equally adorable! Don't let "puppy cuteness" be the only factor in your choice of a pup; behavior and temperament are more important.

41

Neapolitan Mastiff

The Neo puppy will grow into a very large dog. This crate is appropriate for the young Neo, but he will outgrow it quickly as he gets older.

bedding and with a favorite toy placed inside, a crate becomes a cozy pseudo-den for your dog. Like his ancestors, he too will seek out the comfort and retreat of a den—you just happen to be providing him with something a little more luxurious than what his early ancestors enjoyed.

As far as purchasing a crate, the type that you buy is up to you. It will most likely be one of the two most popular types: wire or fiberglass. There are advantages and disadvantages to each type. For example, a wire crate is more

CRATE-TRAINING TIPS

During crate training, you should partition off the section of the crate in which the pup stays. If he is given too big an area, this will hinder your training efforts. Crate training is based on the fact that a dog does not like to soil his sleeping quarters, so it is ineffective to keep a pup in a crate that is so big that he can elimi-nate in one end and get far enough away from it to sleep. Also, you want to make the crate den-like for the pup. Blankets and a favorite toy will make the crate cozy for the small pup; as he grows, you may want to evict some of his "roommates" to make more room. It will take some coaxing at first, but be patient. Given some time to get used to it, your pup will adapt to his new home-within-a-home quite nicely.

PHOTO COURTESY OF DOSKOCIL.

open, allowing the air to flow through and affording the dog a view of what is going on around him while a fiberglass crate is sturdier. Both can double as travel crates, providing protection for

Purchase the largest crate possible.

43

the dog. The size of the crate is another thing to consider. Puppies do not stay puppies forever—in fact, sometimes it seems as if they grow right before your eyes. A medium-size crate may be fine for a very young Neapolitan Mastiff pup, but it will not do him much good for long! Unless you have the money and the inclination to buy a new crate every time your pup has a growth spurt, it is better to get one that will accommodate your dog both as a pup and at full size. An extra-large crate will be necessary for a full-grown Neapolitan Mastiff, who stands approximately 26 to 29 inches high.

QUALITY FOOD

The cost of food must be mentioned. All dogs need a good-quality food with an adequate supply of protein to develop their bones and muscles properly. Most dogs are not picky eaters but, unless fed properly, can quickly succumb to skin problems.

BEDDING

A crate pad and blanket in the dog's crate will help the dog feel more at home. This will take the place of the leaves, twigs, etc., that the pup would use in the wild to make a den; the pup can

Your Neo puppy should have soft bedding or a blanket with which to snuggle. He needs something warm and cuddly to replace the warmth of his mother and littermates.

make his own "burrow" in the crate. Although your pup is far removed from his den-making ancestors, the denning instinct is still a part of his genetic makeup. Second, until you bring your pup home, he has been sleeping amid the warmth of his mother and littermates, and while a blanket is not the same as a warm, breathing body, it still provides heat and something with which to snuggle. You will want to wash your pup's bedding frequently in case he has an accident in his crate, and replace or remove any blanket that becomes ragged and starts to fall apart.

Toys

Toys are a must for dogs of all ages, especially for curious playful pups. Puppies are the "children" of the dog world, and what child does not love toys? Chew toys provide enjoyment to both dog and owner—your dog will enjoy playing with his favorite toys, while you will enjoy the fact that they distract him from your expensive shoes and leather sofa. Puppies love to chew; in fact, chewing is a physical need for pups as they are teething, and everything looks appetizing! The full range of your possessions—from old dishcloth to Oriental rug—are fair game in the eyes of a teething pup. Puppies are not all that discerning when it comes to finding something to literally

"sink their teeth into"—everything tastes great!

Neapolitan Mastiff puppies are fairly aggressive chewers and only the hardest, strongest toys should be offered to them. Breeders advise owners to resist stuffed toys, because they can become de-stuffed in no time. The overly excited pup may ingest the stuffing, which is neither digestible nor nutritious.

Similarly, squeaky toys are quite popular, but must be avoided for the Neapolitan Mastiff. Perhaps a squeaky toy can be used as an aid in training, but not for free play. If a pup "disembowels" one of these, the small plastic squeaker inside can be

TOYS, TOYS, TOYS!

With a big variety of dog toys available, and so many that look like they would be a lot of fun for a dog, be careful in your selection. It is amazing what a set of puppy teeth can do to an innocent-looking toy; so, obviously, safety is a major consideration. Be sure to choose the most durable products that you can find. Hard nylon bones and toys are a safe bet, and many of them are offered in different scents and flavors that will be sure to capture your dog's attention. It is always fun to play a game of fetch with your dog, and there are balls and flying discs that are specially made to withstand dog teeth.

45

Your local pet shop certainly has a wide variety of toys to keep your Neo occupied. Only use very strong toys that have been designed for dogs. *Never* use toys designed for humans.

dangerous if swallowed. Monitor the condition of all your pup's toys carefully and get rid of any that have been chewed to the point of becoming potentially dangerous.

Teething pups can destroy ordinary flying discs in short order; fortunately, there are similar products that are specifically made for dogs to withstand chewing.

Be careful of natural bones, which have a tendency to splinter into sharp, dangerous pieces. Also be careful of rawhide, which can turn into pieces that are easy to swallow or into a mushy mess on your carpet.

LEAD
A nylon lead is probably the best option as it is the most resistant to puppy teeth should your pup take a liking to chewing on his lead. Of course, this is a habit that should be nipped in the bud, but if your pup likes to chew on his lead he has a very slim chance of being able to chew through the strong nylon. Nylon leads are also light-

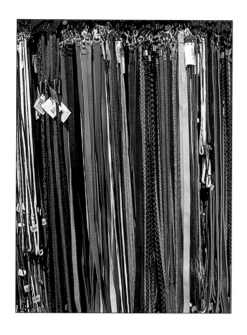

it, and, of course, you have to attach the lead to something! A lightweight nylon collar is a good choice; make sure that it fits snugly enough so that the pup cannot wriggle out of it, but is loose enough so that it will not be uncomfortably tight around the pup's neck. You should be able to fit a finger between the pup and the collar. It may take some time for your pup to get used to wearing the collar, but soon he will not even notice that it is there. When your Neapolitan is full-grown he may require a stronger leather collar, which should be readily available at a local pet shop. There are also manufacturers who specialize in products designed just for larger dogs; their merchandise is often available at pet shops

Your local pet shop should have a wide variety of leads from which you can choose. You need a strong, heavy lead for an adult Neapolitan Mastiff, but you can start your puppy off with something lighter.

weight, which is good for a young Neapolitan Mastiff who is just getting used to the idea of walking on a lead. For everyday walking and safety purposes, the nylon lead is a good choice. Of course there are special leads for training purposes, and specially made leather harnesses for the working Neapolitan Mastiffs, but these are not necessary for routine walks. However, you may consider purchasing a stronger leather lead for your formidably-sized Neapolitan.

COLLAR
Your pup should get used to wearing a collar all the time since you will want to attach his ID tags to

FINANCIAL RESPONSIBILITY

Grooming tools, collars, leashes, crate, dog beds and, of course, toys will be expenses to you when you first obtain your pup, and the cost will continue throughout your dog's lifetime. If your puppy damages or destroys your possessions (as most puppies surely will!) or something belonging to a neighbor, you can calculate additional expense. There is also flea and pest control, which every dog owner faces more than once. You must be able to handle the financial responsibility of owning a dog.

47

The collar you select for your Neo puppy should be expandable to accommodate him as he grows.

Allow your pup some time to get used to the feeling of having the lead attached to the collar.

and water bowls on a specially made elevated stand; this brings the food closer to the dog's level so he does not have to crane his neck to reach his bowls, thus aiding his digestion and helping to guard against bloat or gastric torsion. It is important to buy sturdy bowls since anything is in danger of being chewed by puppy teeth and you do not want your dog to be constantly chewing apart his bowl (for his safety and for your bank account!).

CLEANING SUPPLIES
Until a pup is house-trained, you will be doing a lot of cleaning. Accidents will occur, which is

or through the mail. Choke collars are made for training, but should only be used by an experienced handler.

FOOD AND WATER BOWLS
Your pup will need two bowls, one for food and one for water. You may want two sets of bowls, one for inside and one for outside, depending on where the dog will be fed and where he will be spending most of his time. Stainless steel or sturdy plastic bowls are popular choices. Plastic bowls are more chewable. Dogs tend not to chew on the steel variety, which can be sterilized. Some dog owners like to put their dogs' food

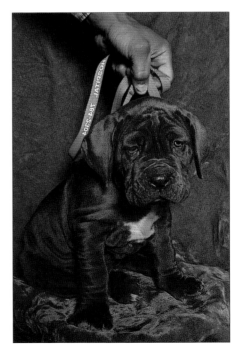

The BUCKLE COLLAR is the standard collar used for everyday purposes. Be sure that you adjust the buckle on growing puppies. Check it every day. It can become too tight overnight! These collars can be made of leather or nylon. Attach your dog's identification tags to this collar.

The CHOKE COLLAR is the usual collar recommended for training. It is constructed of highly polished steel so that it slides easily through the stainless steel loop. The idea is that the dog controls the pressure around his neck and he will stop pulling if the collar becomes uncomfortable. Never leave a choke collar on your dog when not training.

The HALTER is for a trained dog that has to be restrained to prevent running away, chasing a cat and the like. Considered the most humane of all collars, it is frequently used on smaller dogs on which collars are not comfortable.

okay in the beginning because the puppy does not know any better. All you can do is be prepared to clean up any "accidents." Old rags, towels, newspapers and a safe disinfectant are good to have on hand.

BEYOND THE BASICS

The items previously discussed are the bare necessities. You will find out what else you need as you go along—grooming supplies, flea/tick protection, baby gates to partition a room, etc. These things will vary depending on your situation but it is important that you have everything you need to feed and make your Neapolitan Mastiff comfortable in his first few days at home.

A variety of dog bowls for food and water can be found at your local pet shop.

PUPPY-PROOFING YOUR HOME

Aside from making sure that your Neapolitan Mastiff will be comfortable in your home, you also have to make sure that your

SKULL & CROSSBONES

Thoroughly puppy-proof your house before bringing your puppy home. Never use cockroach or rodent poisons or plant fertilizers in any area accessible to the puppy. Avoid the use of toilet cleaners. Most dogs are born with "toilet-bowl sonar" and will take a drink if the lid is left open. Also keep the trash secured and out of reach.

home is safe for your Neapolitan Mastiff. This means taking precautions that your pup will not get into anything he should not get into and that there is nothing within his reach that may harm him should he sniff it, chew it, inspect it, etc. This probably seems obvious since, while you are primarily concerned with your pup's safety, at the same time you do not want your belongings to be ruined. Breakables should be placed out of reach if your dog is to have full run of the house. If he is to be limited to certain places within the house, keep any potentially dangerous items in the "off-limits" areas. An electrical cord can pose a danger should the puppy decide to taste it—and who is going to convince a pup that it would not make a great chew toy? Cords should be fastened tightly against the wall. If your dog is going to spend time in a crate, make sure that there is nothing near his crate that he can reach if he sticks his curious little nose or paws through the openings. Just as you would with a child, keep all household cleaners and chemicals where the pup cannot get to them.

It is also important to make sure that the outside of your home is safe. Of course your puppy should never be unsupervised, but a pup let loose in the yard will want to run and explore, and he should be granted that freedom.

A very useful device for all dog owners is a "poop-scoop." Be a good citizen and clean up after your Neo, even in your own yard.

Do not let a fence give you a false sense of security; you would be surprised how crafty (and persistent) a dog can be in figuring out how to dig under and squeeze his way through small holes, or to jump or climb over a fence. The remedy is to make the fence high enough so that it really is impossi-

CHEMICAL TOXINS

Scour your garage for potential puppy dangers. Remove weed killers, pesticides and antifreeze materials. Antifreeze is highly toxic and a few drops can kill a puppy or an adult dog. The sweet taste attracts the animal, who will quickly consume it from the floor or pavement.

51

know some other Neapolitan Mastiff owners who can suggest a good vet. Either way, you should have an appointment arranged for your pup before you pick him up and plan on taking him for an examination before bringing him home.

The pup's first visit will consist of an overall examination to make sure that the pup does not have any problems that are not apparent to you. The veterinarian will also set up a schedule for the pup's vaccinations; the breeder will inform you of which ones the pup has already received and the vet can continue from there.

INTRODUCTION TO THE FAMILY
Everyone in the house will be excited about the puppy's coming home and will want to pet him

Your house is not the only area to puppy-proof; the yard needs to be safe for your pup as well. Make sure that there are no poisonous plants in the garden and that you do not use harmful chemicals on the grass.

ble for your dog to get over it (about 8 feet should suffice), and well embedded into the ground. Be sure to repair or secure any gaps in the fence. Check the fence periodically to ensure that it is in good shape and make repairs as needed; a very determined pup may return to the same spot to "work on it" until he is able to get through.

FIRST TRIP TO THE VET
You have picked out your puppy, and your home and family are ready. Now all you have to do is collect your Neapolitan Mastiff from the breeder and the fun begins, right? Well…not so fast. Something else you need to prepare is your pup's first trip to the veterinarian. Perhaps the breeder can recommend someone in the area who specializes in large-breed dogs, or maybe you

THE RIDE HOME
Taking your dog from the breeder to your home in a car can be a very uncomfortable experience for both of you. The puppy will have been taken from his warm, friendly, safe environment and brought into a strange new environment—an environment that moves! Be prepared for loose bowels, urination, crying, whining and even fear biting. With proper love and encouragement when you arrive home, the stress of the trip should quickly disappear.

and play with him, but it is best to make the introduction low-key so as not to overwhelm the puppy. He is apprehensive already. It is the first time he has been separated from his mother and the breeder, and the ride to your home is likely the first time he has been in a car. The last thing you want to do is smother him, as this will only frighten him further. This is not to say that human contact is not extremely necessary at this stage, because this is the time when a connection between the pup and his human family is formed. Gentle petting and soothing words should help console him, as well as just putting him down and letting him explore on his own (under your watchful eye, of course).

The pup may approach the family members or may busy

himself with exploring for a while. Gradually, each person should spend some time with the pup, one at a time, crouching down to get as close to the pup's level as possible and letting him sniff their hands and petting him gently. He definitely needs human attention and he needs to be touched—this is how to form an immediate bond. Just remember

that the pup is experiencing a lot of things for the first time, at the same time. There are new people, new noises, new smells and new things to investigate: so be gentle, be affectionate and be as comforting as you can be.

YOUR PUP'S FIRST NIGHT HOME

You have traveled home with your new charge safely in his crate or on a passenger's lap. He's been to the vet for a thorough check-up; he's been weighed, his

You should take your Neo puppy to the vet for a general health evaluation soon after buying him. This is how to get your life with a Neo off to a good start.

PUPPY FEEDING

You will probably start feeding your pup the same food that he has been getting from the breeder; the breeder should give you a few days' supply to start you off. Although you should not give your pup too many treats, you will want to have puppy treats on hand for coaxing, training, rewards, etc. Be careful, though, as a small pup's calorie requirements are relatively low and a few treats can add up to almost a full day's worth of calories without the required nutrition.

Neapolitan Mastiff

Don't overwhelm your puppy in his first day at your home. Give him time to acclimate himself to his new surroundings, while you keep a close eye on his explorations.

papers examined; perhaps he's even been vaccinated and wormed as well. He's met the family and he's licked the whole family, including the excited children and the less-than-happy cat. He's explored his area, his new bed, the yard and anywhere else he's been permitted. He's eaten his first meal at home and relieved himself in the proper place. He's heard lots of new sounds, smelled new friends and seen more of the outside world than ever before.

That was just the first day! He's worn out and is ready for bed…or so you think!

It's puppy's first night and you are ready to say "Good night"— keep in mind that this is puppy's first night ever to be sleeping alone. His dam and littermates are no longer at paw's length and he's a bit scared, cold and lonely. Be reassuring to your new family member. This is not the time to spoil him and give in to his inevitable whining.

Pups learn much about life through play and interacting with their littermates. As the pup's owner, you take over as his pack leader and teacher.

54

Puppies whine. They whine to let the others know where they are and hopefully to get company out of it. Place your pup in his new bed or crate in his room and close the door. Mercifully, he may fall asleep without a peep. When the inevitable occurs, ignore the whining: he is fine. Be strong and keep his interest in mind. Do not allow your heart to become guilty and visit the pup. He will fall asleep.

Many breeders recommend placing a piece of bedding from his former homestead in his new bed so that he recognizes the scent of his littermates. Others still advise placing a hot water bottle in his bed for warmth. This latter may be a good idea provided the pup doesn't attempt to suckle—he'll get good and wet and may not fall asleep so fast.

Puppy's first night can be somewhat stressful for the pup

Your new Neo puppy will needs lots of socialization and loving affection, but letting your pup kiss you on the mouth is not a sanitary practice.

and his new family. Remember that you are setting the tone of night-time at your house. Unless you want to play with your pup every night at 10 p.m., midnight and 2 a.m., don't initiate the habit. Your family will thank you, and so will your pup!

SOCIALIZATION

Thorough socialization includes not only meeting new people but also being introduced to new experiences such as riding in the car, having his coat brushed, hearing the television, walking in a crowd—the list is endless. The more your pup experiences, and the more positive the experiences are, the less of a shock and the less frightening it will be for your pup to encounter new things.

PREVENTING PUPPY PROBLEMS

SOCIALIZATION

Now that you have done all of the preparatory work and have helped your pup get accustomed to his new home and family, it is about time for you to have some fun! Socializing your Neapolitan Mastiff pup gives you the opportunity to show off your new friend, and your pup gets to reap the benefits of being an adorable furry creature that people will want to pet and, in general, think is absolutely irresistable!

Besides getting to know his new family, your puppy should be exposed to other people, animals and situations, but of course he must not come into close contact with dogs you don't know well until his course of injections is fully complete. This will help him become well adjusted as he grows up and less prone to being timid or fearful of the new things he will encounter. Your pup's socialization began at the breeder's but now it is your responsibility to continue it. The socialization he receives up until the age of 12

BOY OR GIRL?

An important consideration to be discussed is the sex of your puppy. For a family companion, a bitch may be the better choice, considering the female's inbred concern for all young creatures and her accompanying tolerance and patience. It is always advisable to spay a pet bitch, which may guarantee her a longer life.

weeks is the most critical, as this is the time when he forms his impressions of the outside world. Be especially careful during the eight-to-ten-week period, also known as the fear period. The

Wandamm della Grotta Azzurra, shown here at 12 weeks of age, is a handsome black male owned by La Tutela Kennels.

interaction he receives during this time should be gentle and reassuring. Lack of socialization can manifest itself in fear and aggression as the dog grows up. He needs lots of human contact, affection, handling and exposure to other animals.

Once your pup has received his necessary vaccinations, feel free to take him out and about (on his lead, of course). Walk him around the neighborhood, take him on your daily errands, let people pet him, let him meet other dogs and pets, etc. Puppies do not have to try to make friends; there will be no shortage of people who will want to introduce themselves. Just make sure that you carefully supervise each meeting. If the neighborhood children want to say hello, for example, that is great—children and pups most often make great companions. Sometimes an excited child can unintentionally handle a pup too roughly, or an overzealous pup can playfully nip a little too hard. You want to make socialization experiences positive ones. What a pup learns during this very formative stage will affect his attitude toward future encounters. You want your dog to be comfortable around everyone. A pup that has a bad experience with a child may grow up to be a dog that is shy around or aggressive toward children.

> ## TRAINING TIP
>
> Training your puppy takes much patience and can be frustrating at times, but you should see results from your efforts. If you have a puppy that seems untrainable, take him to a trainer or behaviorist. The dog may have a personality problem that requires the help of a professional, or perhaps you need help in learning how to train your dog.

CONSISTENCY IN TRAINING

Dogs, being pack animals, naturally need a leader, or else they try to establish dominance in their packs. When you bring a dog into your family, the choice of who becomes the leader and who becomes the "pack" is entirely up to you! Your pup's intuitive quest for dominance, coupled with the fact that it is nearly impossible to look at an adorable Neapolitan Mastiff pup, with his wrinkly face, and not cave in, give the pup almost an unfair advantage in getting the upper hand! A pup will definitely test the waters to see what he can and cannot do. Do not give in to those pleading eyes—stand your ground when it comes to disciplining the pup and make sure that all family members do the same. It will only confuse the pup when Mother tells him to get off the sofa when he is used to sitting up there with Father to

in a young developing pup than to wait until the pup's bad behavior becomes the adult dog's bad habit. There are some problems that are especially prevalent in puppies as they develop.

NIPPING

As puppies start to teethe, they feel the need to sink their teeth into anything available...unfortunately that includes your fingers, arms, hair, and toes. You may find this behavior cute for the first five seconds... until you feel just how sharp those puppy teeth are. This is something you want to discourage immediately and consistently with a firm "No!"

It's up to you to decide if you want to allow your dog on the furniture. Once your Neo reaches full size, he may not leave any room on the sofa for you!

watch the nightly news. Avoid discrepancies by having all members of the household decide on the rules before the pup even comes home...and be consistent in enforcing them! Early training shapes the dog's personality, so you cannot be unclear in what you expect.

COMMON PUPPY PROBLEMS

The best way to prevent puppy problems is to be proactive in stopping an undesirable behavior as soon as it starts. The old saying "You can't teach an old dog new tricks" does not necessarily hold true, but it is true that it is much easier to discourage bad behavior

PUPPY PROBLEMS

The majority of problems that are commonly seen in young pups will disappear as your dog gets older. However, how you deal with problems when he is young will determine how he reacts to discipline as an adult dog. It is important to establish who is boss (hopefully it will be you!) right away when you are first bonding with your dog. This bond will set the tone for the rest of your life together.

CHEWING TIPS

Chewing goes hand in hand with nipping in the sense that a teething puppy is always looking for a way to soothe his aching gums. In this case, instead of chewing on you, he may have taken a liking to your favorite shoe or something else which he should not be chewing. Again, realize that this is a normal canine behavior that does not need to be discouraged, only redirected. Your pup just needs to be taught what is acceptable to chew on and what is off-limits. Consistently tell him "No!" when you catch him chewing on something forbidden and give him a chew toy.

Conversely, praise him when you catch him chewing on something appropriate. In this way you are discouraging the inappropriate behavior and reinforcing the desired behavior. The puppy's chewing should stop after his adult teeth have come in, but an adult dog continues to chew for various reasons—perhaps because he is bored, needs to relieve tension or just likes to chew. That is why it is important to redirect his chewing when he is still young.

(or whatever number of firm "Nos" it takes for him to understand that you mean business). Then replace your finger with an appropriate chew toy. While this behavior is merely annoying

when the dog is young, it can become dangerous as your Neapolitan Mastiff's adult teeth grow in and his jaws develop if he continues to think it is okay to gnaw on human appendages. Your Neapolitan Mastiff does not mean any harm with a friendly nip, but he also does not know his own amazing strength.

Part of the socialization process is allowing your Neo puppy to meet other dogs and pets. This should always be done under your supervision.

Neapolitan Mastiff

The first few days in your home are somewhat scary for a young pup; they are an adjustment period for him. Make the transition as smooth as possible with gentle handling, attention and affection.

CRYING/WHINING

Your pup will often cry, whine, whimper, howl or make some type of commotion when he is left alone. This is basically his way of calling out for attention to make sure that you know he is there and that you have not forgotten about him. He feels insecure when he is left alone, when you are out of the house and he is in his crate or when you are in another part of the house and he cannot see you. The noise he is making is an expression of the anxiety he feels at being alone, so he needs to be taught that being alone is okay. You are not actually training the dog to stop making noise, you are training him to feel comfortable when he is alone and thus removing the need for him to make the noise. This is where the crate with cozy bedding and a toy comes in handy. You want to know that he is safe when you are not there to supervise, and you know that he will be safe in his crate rather than roaming freely about the house. In order for the pup to stay in his crate without making a fuss, he needs to be comfortable in his crate. On that note, it is extremely important that the crate is never used as a form of punishment, or the pup will have a negative association with the crate.

Accustom the pup to the crate in short, gradually increasing time intervals in which you put him in the crate, maybe with a treat, and stay in the room with him. If he cries or makes a fuss, do not go to him, but stay in his sight. Gradually he will realize that staying in his crate is all right without your help, and it will not be so traumatic for him when you are not there. You may want to leave the radio on softly when you leave the house; the sound of human voices may be comforting to him.

Your Neo cannot be properly trained without using a suitable crate. Once he is used to it, the crate can be used to keep your Neo safe in various situations.

61

DIETARY AND FEEDING CONSIDERATIONS

Neapolitan adults should be fed two times a day and puppies three times a day until they are six months old. Free feeding of the Neapolitan is never recommended. The Neapolitan, from my experience, will consume anywhere from 2 to 6 pounds of dry kibble each day, some individuals eating more or less than others. I am an advocate of feeding either cooked beef, lamb or pork livers, kidneys and hearts and sometimes chicken made into a stew and spooned over the dog's kibble. This constitutes only 10% of the entire meal. I also incorporate vegetables into their diets. Recently, I began adding a porridge made of oats, bran, brown rice and either cracked wheat, barley or blue corn meal to their kibble, while still feeding

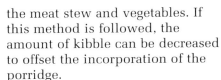

the meat stew and vegetables. If this method is followed, the amount of kibble can be decreased to offset the incorporation of the porridge.

A kibble that is higher in fat and carbohydrates but lower in protein is recommended for the Neapolitan after eight weeks of age. A high-protein diet has been found to contribute to skeletal problems. Too much weight too quickly on a fast-growing puppy like the Neapolitan can cause severe bone and joint deformities and cause him to go down on his pasterns. All puppies are genetically programmed to be a certain size. This size should be reached by providing the puppy with proper nutrition, but it should be noted that a puppy lacking the genes for heavy bone and stockiness can be force-fed and still never achieve the massiveness desired in the Neapolitan.

Today the choices of food for your Neapolitan Mastiff are many and varied. There are simply dozens of brands of food in all sorts of flavors and textures, ranging from puppy diets to those for seniors. There are even hypoallergenic and low-calorie diets available. Because your Neapolitan

STORING DOG FOOD

You must store your dry dog food carefully. Open packages of dog food quickly lose their vitamin value, usually within 90 days of being opened. Mold spores and vermin could also contaminate the food.

Mastiff's food has a bearing on coat, health and temperament, it is essential that the most suitable diet is selected for a Neapolitan Mastiff of his age. It is fair to say, however, that even dedicated owners can be somewhat perplexed by the enormous range of foods available. Only understanding what is best for your dog will help you reach a valued decision.

FOOD PREFERENCE

Selecting the best dry dog food is difficult. There is no majority consensus among veterinary scientists as to the value of nutrient analysis (protein, fat, fiber, moisture, ash, cholesterol, minerals, etc.). All agree that feeding trials are what matter, but you also have to consider the individual dog. The dog's weight, age and activity level, and what pleases his taste, all must be considered. It is probably best to take the advice of your veterinarian. Every dog's dietary requirements vary, even during the lifetime of a particular dog.

If your dog is fed a good dry food, it does not require supplements of meat or vegetables. Dogs do appreciate a little variety in their diets, so you may choose to stay with the same brand but vary the flavor. Alternatively, you may wish to add a little flavored stock to give a difference to the taste.

Dog foods are produced in three basic types: dry, semi-moist and canned. Dry foods are useful for the cost-conscious for overall they tend to be less expensive than semi-moist or canned. These contain the least fat and the most preservatives. In general, canned foods are made up of 60–70% water, while semi-moist ones often contain so much sugar that they are perhaps the least preferred by owners, even though their dogs seem to like them.

A puppy diet is different than an adult diet. Discuss the proper diet for your Neo with your vet or the breeder from whom you purchased the puppy.

63

A PUPPY'S LIFE

Some experts in canine health advise that stress during a dog's early years of development can compromise and weaken his immune system and may trigger the potential for a shortened life expectancy. They emphasize the need for happy and stress-free growing-up years.

Your pup should have a designated area in which he eats his meals; this should be in a place like the kitchen, not your sofa. Do not get in the habit of "catering" to your pup; this puts him in control.

When selecting your dog's diet, three stages of development must be considered: the puppy stage, the adult stage and the senior stage.

PUPPY STAGE

Puppies instinctively want to suck milk from their dam's teats and a normal puppy will exhibit this behavior from just a few moments following birth. If puppies do not attempt to suckle within the first half-hour or so, they should be encouraged to do so by placing them on a nipple, having selected ones with plenty of milk. This early milk supply is important in providing colostrum to protect the puppies during the first eight to ten weeks of their lives. Although a dam's milk is much better than any milk formula, despite there being

While it is preferable to use a proper dog food bowl rather than a pail, you will require something large enough to hold the amount of food required by a growing Neo.

some excellent ones available, if the puppies do not feed the breeder has to feed them himself. For those with less experience, advice from a veterinarian is important so that you feed not only the right quantity of milk but that of correct quality, fed at suitably frequent intervals, usually every two hours during the first few days of life.

Puppies should be allowed to nurse from their dam for about the first six weeks, although from the third or fourth week you will have begun to introduce small portions of suitable solid food. Most breeders like to introduce alternate

GRAIN-BASED DIETS

Some less expensive dog foods are based on grains and other plant proteins. While these products may appear to be attractively priced, many breeders prefer a diet based on animal proteins and believe that they are more conducive to your dog's health. Many grain-based diets rely on soy protein, which may cause flatulence (passing gas).

There are many cases, however, when your dog might require a special diet. These special requirements should only be recommended by your veterinarian.

A litter of Neo pups, still with the breeder. The breeder will keep the pups with their dam until they are weaned. Only after they are fully weaned and eating solid food are they considered old enough to go to new homes.

FEEDING TIPS

• Dog food must be served at room temperature, neither too hot nor too cold. Fresh water, changed daily and served in a clean bowl, is mandatory, especially when feeding dry food.
• Never feed your dog from the table while you are eating, and never feed your dog leftovers from your own meal. They usually contain too much fat and too much seasoning.
• Dogs must chew their food. Hard pellets are excellent; soups and stews are to be avoided.
• Don't add leftovers or any extras to commercial dog food. The normal food is usually balanced, and adding something extra destroys the balance.
• Except for age-related changes, dogs do not require dietary variations. They can be fed the same diet, day after day, without becoming bored or ill

Whether puppy or adult, your Neo's diet will vary depending on how much activity he gets. A more active dog will require more calories, and vice versa.

milk and meat meals initially, building up to weaning time.

By the time the puppies are seven or a maximum of eight weeks old, they should be fully weaned and fed solely on a proprietary puppy food. Selection of the most suitable, good-quality diet at this time is essential for a puppy's fastest growth rate is during the first year of life. Veterinarians are usually able to offer advice in this regard and, the frequency of meals will have been reduced over time. When a young Neapolitan has reached the age of about three months an adult diet can be fed. Neapolitans grow rapidly but don't overfeed your puppy as gaining too much weight too fast can lead to bone and joint problems. Puppy and junior diets should be well balanced for the needs of your dog, so that except in certain circumstances additional vitamins, minerals and proteins will not be required. Protein content should not exceed 24%.

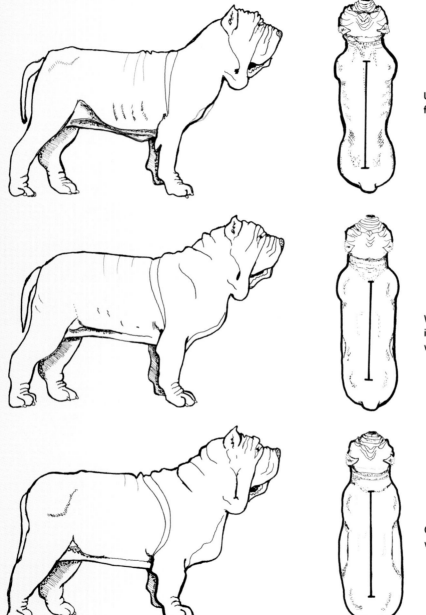

Underweight dog, as shown from the side and top.

Well proportioned dog of ideal weight, top and side views.

Overweight dog, top and side views.

ADULT DIETS

In general the diet of a Neapolitan Mastiff can be changed to an adult one at about three months of age. Again you should rely upon your veterinarian or dietary specialist to recommend an acceptable maintenance diet. Major dog food manufacturers specialize in this type of food, and it is just necessary for you to select the one best suited to your dog's needs. Active dogs may have different requirements than sedate dogs. Neapolitan Mastiffs do well when a small amount (10%) of organ meat is added to their diet. A Neapolitan Mastiff reaches adulthood at about two years of age, though some dogs fully mature at 16 months and others may take up to three-and-a-half years.

SENIOR DIETS

As dogs get older, their metabolism changes. The older dog usually exercises less, moves more slowly and sleeps more. This change in lifestyle and physiological performance requires a change in diet. Since these changes take place slowly, they might not be recognizable. What is easily recognizable is weight gain. By continuing to feed your dog an adult-maintenance diet when he is slowing down metabolically, your dog will gain weight. Obesity in an older dog compounds the health

DO DOGS HAVE TASTE BUDS?

Watching a dog "wolf" or gobble his food, seemingly without chewing, leads an owner to wonder whether his dog can taste anything. Yes, dogs have taste buds, with sensory perception of sweet, salty and sour. Puppies are born with fully mature taste buds.

problems that already accompany old age.

As your dog gets older, few of his organs function up to par. The kidneys slow down and the intestines become less efficient. These age-related factors are best handled with a change in diet and a change in feeding schedule to give smaller portions that are more easily digested.

There is no single best diet for every older dog. While many dogs do well on light or senior diets, other dogs do better on puppy diets or other special premium diets such as lamb and rice. Be sensitive to your senior Neapolitan Mastiff's diet and this will help control other problems that may arise with your old friend.

WATER

The Neapolitan requires large amounts of water and clean, fresh water should always be available. During housebreaking it is necessary to keep an eye on how much water your Neapolitan Mastiff is drinking, but once he is reliably trained he should have access to clean fresh water at all times. Water is just as essential a "nutrient" as anything the dog obtains in his diet. Water keeps the dog's body properly hydrated and promotes normal function of the body's systems.

Water should be changed frequently, at least twice a day, as the Neapolitan deposits a slime in it after drinking, which I compare to the consistency of egg whites. Neapolitans love to drink and with saliva and water dripping from their pendulous lips, they cannot resist the urge to come and put their head on your lap. Towels specifically relegated to the duty of mopping up water and food from the Neapolitan's lips, flews and dewlap seem to do the trick.

ELECTRICAL FENCING

The electrical fencing system which forms an invisible fence works on a battery-operated collar that shocks the dog if it gets too close to the buried (or elevated) wire. There are some people who think very highly of this system of controlling a dog's wandering. Keep in mind that the collar has batteries. For safety's sake, replace the batteries every month with the best quality batteries available.

EXERCISE

All dogs require some form of exercise, regardless of breed. A sedentary lifestyle is as harmful to a dog as it is to a person. The Neapolitan Mastiff is an inactive breed that does not require much exercise, so you definitely do not have to be an athlete to provide your dog with the exercise he needs. Regular walks, play sessions in the yard or letting the dog run free in an enclosed area under your supervision are sufficient forms of exercise for the Neapolitan Mastiff. For those who are more ambitious, you will find that your Neapolitan Mastiff also enjoys long walks. Bear in mind that an overweight dog should never be suddenly over-exercised; instead he should be allowed to increase exercise slowly. Not only is exercise essential to keep the

Your Neo should always have access to water, especially when outside on a hot day. Water should be changed frequently and the water bowl kept clean.

69

routine brushing. Brushing is effective for removing dead hair and stimulating the dog's natural oils to add shine and a healthy look to the coat. The Neapolitan Mastiff's coat is short and dense, and should be brushed weekly as part of routine maintenance. Weekly brushing will get rid of dust and dandruff and remove any dead hair. Regular grooming sessions are also a good way to spend time with your dog. Many dogs grow to like the feel of being brushed and will enjoy the daily routine.

BATHING

Dogs do not need to be bathed as often as humans, but regular bathing is essential for healthy

Teaching your Neo to heel on lead is a necessity or you will find it very difficult to take him for walks. Exercise is important for your dog, just as it is for you.

dog's body fit, it is essential to his mental well-being. A bored dog will find something to do, which often manifests itself in some type of destructive behavior. In this sense, it is essential for the owner's mental well-being as well!

GROOMING

BRUSHING
A natural bristle brush or a hound glove can be used for regular

---

GROOMING EQUIPMENT

How much grooming equipment you purchase will depend on how much grooming you are going to do. Here are some basics:

- Natural bristle brush
- Hound glove
- Metal comb
- Scissors
- Blow dryer
- Rubber mat
- Dog shampoo
- Spray hose attachment
- Ear cleaner
- Cotton balls
- Towels
- Nail clippers

skin and a healthy, shiny coat. The Neapolitan's abundant loose skin requires cleaning and frequent baths. Again, like most anything, if you accustom your pup to being bathed as a puppy, it will be second nature by the time he grows up. You want your dog to be at ease during his bath or else it could end up a wet, soapy, messy ordeal for both of you!

Brush your Neapolitan Mastiff thoroughly before wetting his coat. Make sure that your dog has a good non-slip surface to stand on such as a rubber mat or cement. For an adult Neo, you likely will be undertaking bathing outdoors. Begin by wetting the

BATHING BEAUTY

Once you are sure that the dog is thoroughly rinsed, squeeze the excess water out of his coat with your hand and dry him with a heavy towel. You may choose to use a blow dryer on his coat or just let it dry naturally. In cold weather, never allow your dog outside with a wet coat.

There are "dry bath" products on the market, which are sprays and powders intended for spot cleaning, that can be used between regular baths if necessary. They are not substitutes for regular baths, but they are easy to use for touch-ups as they do not require rinsing.

Your Neo's coat should be brushed on a weekly basis to remove dead hair and to stimulate the skin. Accustom your Neo to routine grooming while he is still a pup.

dog's coat. A hose is necessary for thoroughly wetting and rinsing the coat. Check the water temperature to make sure that it is neither too hot nor too cold.

Next, apply shampoo to the dog's coat and work it into a good lather. You should purchase a shampoo that is made for dogs. Do not use a product made for human hair. Wash the head last; you do not want shampoo to drip into the dog's eyes while you are washing the rest of his body. Work the shampoo all the way down to the skin. You can use this opportunity to check the skin for any bumps, bites or other abnormalities. Do not neglect any area of the body—get all of the hard-to-reach places.

Once the dog has been thoroughly shampooed, he requires an equally thorough rinsing. Shampoo left in the coat can be irritating to the skin. Protect his eyes from the shampoo by shielding them with your hand and directing the flow of water in the opposite direction. You should also avoid getting water in the ear canal. Be prepared for your dog to shake out his coat—you might want to stand back, but make sure you have a hold on the dog to keep him from running away.

EAR CLEANING

The ears should be kept clean and any excess hair inside the ear should be carefully cut. Ears can be cleaned with a cotton ball and special cleaner or ear powder made especially for dogs. Be on the lookout for any signs of infection or ear-mite infestation. If your Neapolitan Mastiff has been shaking his head or scratching at his ears frequently, this usually indicates a problem. If his ears have an unusual odor, this is a sure sign of mite infestation or infection, and a signal to have his ears checked by the veterinarian.

NAIL CLIPPING

Your Neapolitan Mastiff should be accustomed to having his nails trimmed at an early age, since it will be part of your maintenance routine throughout his life. Not only does it look nicer, but long nails can scratch someone unintentionally. Also, a long nail has a better chance of ripping and bleeding, or causing the feet to spread. A good rule of

SOAP IT UP

The use of human soap products like shampoo, bubble bath and hand soap can be damaging to a dog's coat and skin. Human products are too strong; they remove the protective oils coating the dog's hair and skin that make him water-resistant. Use only shampoo made especially for dogs. You may like to use a medicated shampoo, which will help to keep external parasites at bay.

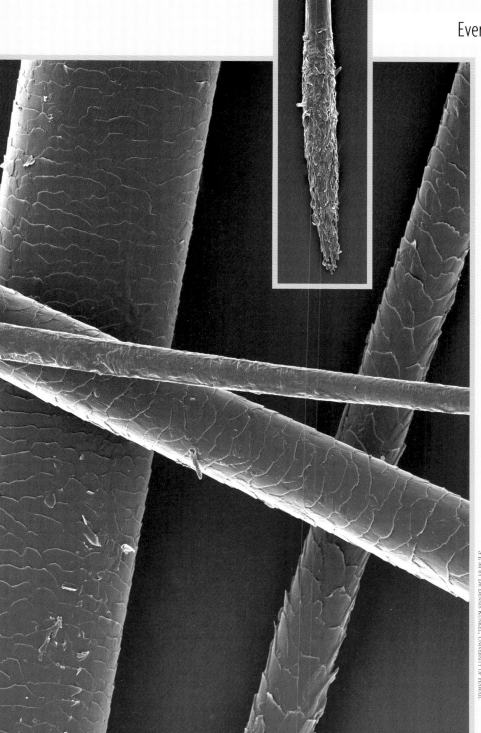

Typical dog's hair with a healthy cuticle (outer covering). The inset shows a hair root. The enlargement is about 175 times natural size (hair root about 38 times). These scanning electron micrographs were prepared by Dr. Dennis Kunkel at the University of Hawaii.

S E M by Dr Dennis Kunkel, University of Hawaii.

73

Your Neo's ears can be cleaned with special wipes available from your local pet shop. Inspect your Neo's ears for ear mites or signs of infection.

thumb is that if you can hear your dog's nails' clicking on the floor when he walks, his nails are too long.

Before you start cutting, make sure you can identify the "quick" in each nail. The quick is a blood vessel that runs through the center of each nail and grows rather close to the end. It will bleed if accidentally cut, which will be quite painful for the dog as it contains nerve endings. Keep

some type of clotting agent on hand, such as a styptic pencil or styptic powder (the type used for shaving). This will stop the bleeding quickly when applied to the end of the cut nail. Do not panic if this happens, just stop the bleeding and talk soothingly to your dog. Once he has calmed down, move on to the next nail. It is better to clip a little at a time, particularly with black-nailed dogs.

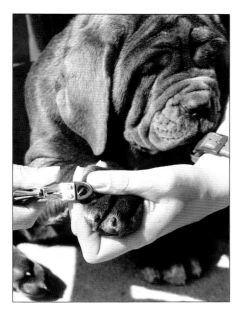

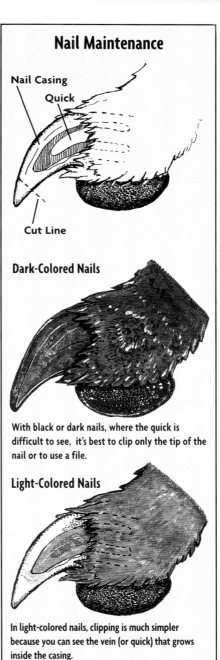

Nail Maintenance

Nail Casing

Quick

Cut Line

Dark-Colored Nails

With black or dark nails, where the quick is difficult to see, it's best to clip only the tip of the nail or to use a file.

Light-Colored Nails

In light-colored nails, clipping is much simpler because you can see the vein (or quick) that grows inside the casing.

Special nail clippers for dogs are available from your local pet shop.

Hold your pup steady as you begin trimming his nails; you do not want him to make any sudden movements or run away. Talk to him soothingly and stroke him as you clip. Holding his foot in your hand, simply take off the end of each nail in one quick clip. You can purchase nail clippers that are specially made for dogs; you can probably find them wherever you buy pet supplies.

TRAVELING WITH YOUR DOG

CAR TRAVEL

You should accustom your Neapolitan Mastiff to riding in a car at an early age. You may or may not take him in the car often, but at the very least he

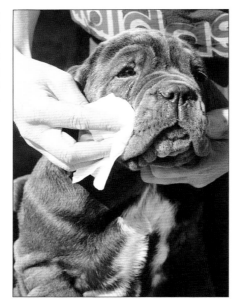

The Neo's loose skin requires special attention. Cleaning between the wrinkles on the face is demonstrated here.

much like a seat belt. Do not let the dog roam loose in the vehicle—this is very dangerous! If you should stop short, your dog can be thrown and injured. If the dog starts climbing on you and pestering you while you are driving, you will not be able to concentrate on the road. It is an unsafe situation for everyone—human and canine.

For long trips, be prepared to stop to let the dog relieve himself. Bring along whatever you need to clean up after him. You should take along some paper towels and perhaps some old bath towels for use should he have an accident in

will need to go to the vet and you do not want these trips to be traumatic for the dog or a big hassle for you. The safest way for a dog to ride in the car is in his crate. If he uses a crate in the house, you can use the same crate for travel, if your vehicle can accommodate it. You may need a van or sports utility vehicle for transporting an adult Neapolitan. Put the pup in the crate and see how he reacts. If the puppy seems uneasy, you can have a passenger hold him on his lap while you drive but you will need to find another solution before your dog is full grown. Another option is a specially made safety harness for dogs, which straps the dog in

TRAVEL TIP

Never leave your dog alone in the car. In hot weather, your dog can die from the high temperature inside a closed vehicle; even a car parked in the shade can heat up very quickly. Leaving the window open is dangerous as well since the dog can hurt himself trying to get out.

ON THE ROAD

If you are going on a long motor trip with your dog, be sure the hotels are dog-friendly. Many hotels do not accept dogs. Also take along some ice that can be thawed and offered to your dog if he becomes over-heated. Most dogs like to lick ice.

the car or suffer from motion sickness. If you are traveling in warm weather, always have water to offer your pet.

AIR TRAVEL

Contact your chosen airline before proceeding with your travel plans that include your Neo. The dog will be required to travel in a fiberglass crate and you should always check in advance with the airline regarding specific requirements for the crate's size, type and labeling. To help put the dog at ease, give him one of his favorite toys in the crate. Do not feed the dog for several hours prior to checking in so that you minimize his need to relieve himself. However, some airlines require that the dog must be fed within four hours of arriving at the airport, in which case a light meal is best. For long trips, you will have to attach food and water bowls to the dog's crate so that airline employees can tend to him between legs of the trip.

Make sure your dog is properly identified and that your contact information appears on his ID tags and on his crate. Animals travel in a different area of the plane than human passengers so every rule must be strictly adhered to so as to prevent the risk of getting separated from your dog.

Whenever you must crate your dog, he should always be allowed out on a regular basis so he can relieve himself.

BOARDING AND VACATIONS

So you want to take a family vacation—and you want to include *all* members of the family. You would probably make arrangements for accommodations ahead of time anyway, but this is especially important when traveling with a dog. You

77

TRAVELING ABROAD

For international travel you will have to make arrangements well in advance (perhaps months), as countries' regulations pertaining to bringing in animals differ. There may be special health certificates and/or vaccinations that your dog will need before taking the trip; sometimes this has to be done within a certain time frame. In rabies-free countries, you will need to bring proof of the dog's rabies vaccination and there may be a quarantine period upon arrival.

do not want to make an overnight stop at the only place around for miles and find out that they do not allow dogs. Also, you do not want to reserve a place for your family without confirming that you are traveling with a dog because if it is against their policy you may not have a place to stay.

Alternatively, if you are traveling and choose not to bring your Neapolitan Mastiff, you will have to make arrangements for him while you are away. Some options are to take him to a neighbor's house to stay while you are gone, to have a trusted friend stop by often or stay at your house, or bring your dog to a reputable boarding kennel. If you choose to board him at a kennel, you should visit in advance to see the facility, how clean they are and where the dogs are kept. Talk to some of the employees and see how they treat the dogs—do they spend time with the dogs, play with them, exercise them, etc.? Also find out the kennel's policy on vaccinations and what they require. This is for all of the dogs' safety, since when dogs are kept together, there is a greater risk of diseases being passed from dog to dog.

IDENTIFICATION
Your Neapolitan Mastiff is your valued companion and friend.

That is why you always keep a close eye on him and you have made sure that he cannot escape from the yard or wriggle out of his collar and run away from you. However, accidents can happen and there may come a time when your dog unexpectedly gets separated from you. If this unfortunate event should occur, the first thing on your mind will be finding him. Proper identification, including an ID tag, a tattoo, and possibly a microchip, will increase the chances of his being returned to you safely and quickly.

IDENTIFICATION OPTIONS

As puppies become more and more expensive, especially those puppies of high quality for showing and/or breeding, they have a greater chance of being stolen. The usual collar dog tag is, of course, easily removed. But there are two more permanent techniques that have become widely used for identification.

The puppy microchip implantation involves the injection of a small microchip, about the size of a corn kernel, under the skin of the dog. If your dog shows up at a clinic or shelter, or is offered for resale under less-than-savory circumstances, it can be positively identified by the microchip. The microchip is scanned, and a registry quickly identifies you as the owner.

Tattooing is done on various parts of the dog, from his belly to his cheeks. The number tattooed can be your telephone number or any other number that you can easily memorize. When professional dog thieves see a tattooed dog, they usually lose interest. Both microchipping and tattooing can be done at your local veterinary clinic. For the safety of our dogs, no laboratory facility or dog broker will accept a tattooed dog as stock.

Discuss microchipping and tattooing with your veterinarian and breeder. Some vets perform these services on their own premises for a reasonable fee. Be certain that the dog do is then properly registered with a legitimate national database.

If you are searching for a boarding kennel, look for one that is clean, with sufficient space to enable the Neo to walk around and get some exercise.

79

TRAINING YOUR
NEAPOLITAN MASTIFF

Living with an untrained dog is a lot like owning a piano that you do not know how to play—it is a nice object to look at but it does not do much more than that to bring you pleasure. Now try taking piano lessons and suddenly the piano comes alive and brings forth magical sounds and rhythms that set your heart singing and your body swaying.

The same is true with your Neapolitan Mastiff. Any dog is a big responsibility and if not trained sensibly may develop unacceptable behavior that annoys you or could even cause family friction.

To train your Neapolitan Mastiff, you may like to enroll in an obedience class. Teach him good manners as you learn how and why he behaves the way he does. Find out how to communicate with your dog and how to recognize and understand his communications with you. Suddenly the dog takes on a new role in your life—he is smart, interesting, well behaved and fun to be with. He demonstrates his bond of devotion to you daily. In other words, your Neapolitan Mastiff does wonders for your ego because he constantly reminds you that you are not only his leader, you are his hero!

Those involved with teaching dog obedience and counseling owners about their dogs' behavior have discovered some interesting facts about dog ownership. For example, training dogs when they are puppies results in the highest rate of success in developing well-mannered and well-adjusted adult dogs. Training an older dog, from six months to six years of age, can produce almost equal results providing that the owner accepts

REAP THE REWARDS

If you start with a normal, healthy dog and give him time, patience and some carefully executed lessons, you will reap the rewards of that training for the life of the dog. And what a life it will be! The two of you will find immeasurable pleasure in the companionship you have built together with love, respect and understanding.

the dog's slower rate of learning capability and is willing to work patiently to help the dog succeed at developing to his fullest potential. Unfortunately, many owners of untrained adult dogs lack the patience factor, so they do not persist until their dogs are successful at learning particular behaviors.

Training a puppy, aged 10 to 16 weeks (20 weeks at the most), is like working with a dry sponge in a pool of water. The pup soaks up whatever you show him and constantly looks for more things to do and learn. At this early age, his body is not yet producing hormones, and therein lies the reason for such a high rate of success. Without hormones, he is focused on his owners and not particularly interested in investigating other places, dogs, people, etc. You are his leader: his provider of food, water, shelter and security. He latches onto you and wants to stay close. He will usually follow you from room to room, will not let you out of his sight when you are outdoors with him, and will respond in like manner to the people and animals you encounter. If you greet a friend warmly, he will be happy to greet the person as well. If, however, you are hesitant, even anxious, about the approach of a stranger, he will respond accordingly.

Once the puppy begins to produce hormones, his natural curiosity emerges and he begins to investigate the world around him. It is at this time when you may notice that the untrained dog begins to wander away from you and even ignore your commands to stay close.

There are usually classes within a reasonable distance of the owner's home, but you also

If you have a securely fenced garden, you may choose to feed your Neo outdoors. An advantage is that the dog will have immediate access to his relief area when he is finished eating.

PARENTAL GUIDANCE

Training a dog is a life experience. Many parents admit that much of what they know about raising children they learned from caring for their dogs. Dogs respond to love, fairness and guidance, just as children do. Become a good dog owner and you may become an even better parent.

81

Grass is the most common outdoor surface for Neos. The instinct to relieve themselves on grass is inherited from their well-trained parents.

must put in the time between sessions to practice with your Neapolitan at home. Sometimes there are classes available but the tuition is too costly. Whatever the circumstances, the solution to your training problems lies within the pages of this book.

This chapter is devoted to helping you train your Neapolitan Mastiff at home. If the recommended procedures are followed faithfully, you may expect positive results that will prove rewarding to you and your dog.

Whether your new charge is a puppy or a mature adult, the methods of teaching and the techniques we use in training basic behaviors are the same. After all, no dog, whether puppy or adult, likes harsh or inhumane methods. All creatures, however, respond favorably to gentle motivational methods and sincere praise and encouragement.

HOUSEBREAKING

You can train a puppy to relieve himself wherever you choose, but this must be somewhere suitable. You should bear in mind from the outset that when your puppy is old enough to go out in public places, any canine droppings must be removed at once. You will always have to carry with you a small plastic bag or "poop-scoop."

Outdoor training includes such surfaces as grass, dirt and cement. Indoor training usually means training your dog to newspaper. When deciding on the surface and location that you will want your Neapolitan Mastiff to use, be sure it is going to be permanent. Training your dog to grass and then changing your mind two months later is extremely difficult for both dog and owner.

Next, choose the command you will use each and every time

MEALTIME

Mealtime should be a peaceful time for your puppy. Do not put his food and water bowls in a high-traffic area in the house. For example, give him his own little corner of the kitchen where he can eat undisturbed and where he will not be underfoot. Do not allow small children or other family members to disturb the pup when he is eating.

CALM DOWN

Dogs will do anything for your attention. If you reward the dog when he is calm and resting, you will develop a well-mannered dog. If, on the other hand, you greet your dog excitedly and encourage him to wrestle with you, the dog will greet you the same way and you will have a hyperactive dog on your hands.

you want your puppy to void. "Go hurry up" and "Potty time" are examples of commands commonly used by dog owners.

Get in the habit of giving the puppy your chosen relief command before you take him out. That way, when he becomes an adult, you will be able to determine if he wants to go out when you ask him. A confirmation will be signs of interest, such as wagging his tail, watching you intently, going to the door, etc.

PUPPY'S NEEDS

The puppy needs to relieve himself after play periods, after each meal, after he has been sleeping and any time he indicates that he is looking for a place to urinate or defecate.

The urinary and intestinal tract muscles of very young puppies are not fully developed. Therefore, like human babies, puppies need to relieve themselves frequently.

Take your puppy out often— every hour for an eight-week-old, for example, and always immediately after sleeping and eating. The older the puppy, the less often he will need to relieve himself. Finally, as a mature healthy adult, he will require only three to five relief trips per day.

HOUSING

Since the types of housing and control you provide for your

You can train your Neo to relieve himself in whatever area and on whatever type of surface you choose. Make your choice carefully, as once he is trained you will have a hard time convincing him to go elsewhere.

Clean up after your Neo. Your local pet shop should have a poop-scoop device to assist you in this task.

83

Do not get in the habit of carrying your pup to his relief area. Take him there on lead and keep visits to the relief site as short as possible.

voice, watching you while you are doing things and smelling you nearby are all positive reinforcers that he is now a member of your pack. Usually a family room, the kitchen or a nearby adjoining breakfast area is ideal for providing safety and security for both puppy and owner.

Within that room there should be a smaller area which the puppy can call his own. An alcove, a wire or fiberglass dog crate or a gated corner from which he can view the activities of his new family will be fine. The size of the area or crate is the key factor here. The area must be large enough for the puppy to lie down and stretch out as well as stand up without rubbing his head on the top, yet small enough so that he cannot

puppy has a direct relationship on the success of house-training, we consider the various aspects of both before we begin training.

Bringing a new puppy home and turning him loose in your house can be compared to turning a child loose in a sports arena and telling the child that the place is all his! The sheer enormity of the place would be too much for him to handle.

Instead, offer the puppy clearly defined areas where he can play, sleep, eat and live. A room of the house where the family gathers is the most obvious choice. Puppies are social animals and need to feel a part of the pack right from the start. Hearing your

PAPER CAPER

Never line your pup's sleeping area with newspaper. Puppy litters are usually raised on newspaper and, once in your home, the puppy will immediately associate newspaper with voiding. Never put newspaper on any floor while house-training, as this will only confuse the puppy. If you are paper-training him, use paper in his designated relief area only. Finally, restrict water intake after evening meals. Offer a few licks at a time—never let a young puppy gulp water after meals.

CANINE DEVELOPMENT SCHEDULE

It is important to understand how and at what age a puppy develops into adulthood. If you are a puppy owner, consult the following Canine Development Schedule to determine the stage of development your puppy is currently experiencing. This knowledge will help you as you work with the puppy in the weeks and months ahead.

Period	Age	Characteristics
FIRST TO THIRD	BIRTH TO SEVEN WEEKS	Puppy needs food, sleep and warmth, and responds to simple and gentle touching. Needs mother for security and disciplining. Needs littermates for learning and interacting with other dogs. Pup learns to function within a pack and learns pack order of dominance. Begin socializing with adults and children for short periods. Begins to become aware of his environment.
FOURTH	EIGHT TO TWELVE WEEKS	Brain is fully developed. Needs socializing with outside world. Remove from mother and littermates. Needs to change from canine pack to human pack. Human dominance necessary. Fear period occurs between 8 and 16 weeks. Avoid fright and pain.
FIFTH	THIRTEEN TO SIXTEEN WEEKS	Training and formal obedience should begin. Less association with other dogs, more with people, places, situations. Period will pass easily if you remember this is pup's change-to-adolescence time. Be firm and fair. Flight instinct prominent. Permissiveness and over-disciplining can do permanent damage. Praise for good behavior.
JUVENILE	FOUR TO EIGHT MONTHS	Another fear period about 7 to 8 months of age. It passes quickly, but be cautious of fright and pain. Sexual maturity reached. Dominant traits established. Dog should understand sit, down, come and stay by now.

NOTE: THESE ARE APPROXIMATE TIME FRAMES. ALLOW FOR INDIVIDUAL DIFFERENCES IN PUPPIES.

THE GOLDEN RULE

The golden rule of dog training is simple. For each "question" (command), there is only one correct answer (reaction). One command =

one reaction. Keep practicing the command until the dog reacts correctly without hesitating. Be repetitive but not monotonous. Dogs get bored just as people do!

relieve himself at one end and sleep at the other without coming into contact with his droppings until fully trained to relieve himself outside. The designated area should be lined with clean bedding and a toy. Water must always be available, in a non-spill container.

Dogs are, by nature, clean animals and will not remain close to their relief areas unless forced to do so. In those cases, they then become dirty dogs and usually remain that way for life.

CONTROL

By *control*, we mean helping the puppy to create a lifestyle pattern that will be compatible to that of his human pack (*you!*). Just as we guide little children to learn our way of life, we must show the puppy when it is time to play, eat, sleep, exercise and even entertain himself.

Your puppy should always sleep in his crate. He should also learn that, during times of household confusion and excessive human activity such as at breakfast when family members are preparing for the day, he can play by himself in relative safety and comfort in his designated area. Each time you leave the puppy alone, he should understand exactly where he is to stay. You can gradually increase the time he is left alone to get him used to it.

Puppies are chewers. They cannot tell the difference between lamp cords, television wires, shoes, table legs, etc. Chewing into a television wire, for example, can be fatal to the puppy while a shorted wire can start a fire in the house.

Whether housebreaking or teaching basic commands, puppies are most trainable at an early age. The training they receive and the things they experience when very young will leave a lasting impact throughout their lives.

If the puppy chews on the arm of the chair when he is alone, you will probably disci-pline him angrily when you get home. Thus, he makes the asso-ciation that your coming home means he is going to be punished. (He will not remember chewing up the chair and is incapable of making the associa-tion of the discipline with his naughty deed.)

Other times of excitement, such as family parties, visits, etc., can be fun for the puppy provid-ing he can view the activities from the security of his designated area. He is not underfoot and he is not being fed all sorts of titbits that will probably cause him stomach distress, yet he still feels a part of the fun.

A wire crate is fine for inside your home. For a puppy who is not yet house-trained, never put the water bowl inside the crate. This invites accidents when the puppy is crated.

TAKE THE LEAD

Do not carry your dog to his relief area. Lead him there on a leash or, better yet, encourage him to follow you to the spot. If you start carrying him to his spot, you might end up doing this routine forever and your dog will have the satisfaction of having trained *you*.

SCHEDULE

A puppy should be taken to his relief area each time he is released from his designated area, after meals, after a play session, when he first awakens in the morning (at age eight weeks, this can mean

5 a.m.!). The puppy will indicate that he's ready "to go" by circling or sniffing busily—do not misinterpret these signs. For a puppy less than ten weeks of age, a routine of taking him out every hour is necessary. As the puppy grows, he will be able to wait for longer periods of time.

Keep trips to his relief area short. Stay no more than five or six minutes and then return to the house. If he goes during that time, praise him lavishly and take him indoors immediately. If

An important step in housebreaking is teaching the difference between play-time and potty time. The pup will learn to relieve himself quickly so that playtime can begin.

HOW MANY TIMES A DAY?

AGE	RELIEF TRIPS
To 14 weeks	10
14–22 weeks	8
22–32 weeks	6
Adulthood	4
(dog stops growing)	

These are estimates, of course, but they are a guide to the minimum number of opportunities a dog should have each day to relieve himself.

he does not, but he has an accident when you go back indoors, pick him up immediately, say "No! No!" and return to his relief area. Wait a few minutes, then return to the house again. Never hit a puppy or put his face in urine or excrement when he has an accident!

Once indoors, put the puppy in his crate until you have had time to clean up his accident. Then release him to the family area and watch him more closely than before. Chances are, his accident was a result of your not picking up his signal or waiting too long before offering him the opportunity to relieve himself. Never hold a grudge against the puppy for accidents.

Let the puppy learn that going outdoors means it is time to relieve himself, not play. Once trained, he will be able to play indoors and out and still differentiate between the times for play versus the times for relief.

Help him develop regular hours for naps, being alone, playing by himself and just resting, all in his crate. Encourage him to entertain himself while you are busy with your activities. Let him learn that having you near is comforting, but it is not your main purpose in life to provide him with undivided attention.

Each time you put a puppy in his own area, use the same

THE CLEAN LIFE

By providing sleeping and resting quarters that fit the dog, and offering frequent opportunities to relieve himself outside his quarters, the puppy quickly learns that the outdoors (or the newspaper if you are training him to paper) is the place to go when he needs to urinate or defecate. It also reinforces his innate desire to keep his sleeping quarters clean. This, in turn, helps develop the muscle control that will eventually produce a dog with clean living habits.

command, whatever suits best. Soon, he will run to his crate or special area when he hears you say those words.

Crate training provides safety for you, the puppy and the home. It also provides the puppy with a feeling of security, and that helps the puppy achieve self-confidence and clean habits.

Remember that one of the primary ingredients in house-training your puppy is control. Regardless of your lifestyle, there will always be occasions when you will need to have a place where your dog can stay and be happy and safe. Crate training is the answer for now and in the future.

In conclusion, a few key elements are really all you need for a successful house-training method—consistency, frequency, praise, control and supervision. By following these procedures with a normal, healthy puppy, you and the puppy will soon be past the stage of "acci-dents" and ready to move on to a full and rewarding life together.

ROLES OF DISCIPLINE, REWARD AND PUNISHMENT
Discipline, training one to act in accordance with rules, brings

THE SUCCESS METHOD

Success that comes by luck is usually short-lived. Success that comes by well-thought-out proven methods is often more easily achieved and permanent. This is the Success Method. It is designed to give you, the puppy owner, a simple yet proven way to help your puppy develop clean living habits and a feeling of security in his new environment.

6 Steps to Successful Crate Training

1 Tell the puppy "Crate time!" and place him in the crate with a small treat (a piece of cheese or half of a biscuit). Let him stay in the crate for five minutes while you are in the same room. Then release him and praise lavishly. Never release him when he is fussing. Wait until he is quiet before you let him out.

2 Repeat Step 1 several times a day.

3 The next day, place the puppy in the crate as before. Let him stay there for ten minutes. Do this several times.

4 Continue building time in five-minute increments until the puppy stays in his crate for 30 minutes with you in the room. Always take him to his relief area after prolonged periods in his crate.

5 Now go back to Step 1 and let the puppy stay in his crate for five minutes, this time while you are out of the room.

6 Once again, build crate time in five-minute increments with you out of the room. When the puppy will stay willingly in his crate (he may even fall asleep!) for 30 minutes with you out of the room, he will be ready to stay in it for several hours at a time.

order to life. It is as simple as that. Without discipline, particularly in a group society, chaos reigns supreme and the group will eventually perish. Humans and canines are social animals and need some form of discipline in order to function effectively. They must procure food, reproduce to keep the species going and protect their home base and their young.

If there were no discipline in the lives of social animals, they would eventually die from starvation and/or predation by other stronger animals. In the case of domestic canines, dogs need discipline in their lives in order to understand how their pack (you and other family members) functions and how they must act in order to survive.

A large humane society in a highly populated area recently surveyed dog owners regarding their satisfaction with their relationships with their dogs. People who had trained their dogs were 75% more satisfied with their pets than those who had never trained their dogs.

Dr. Edward Thorndike, a noted psychologist, established *Thorndike's Theory of Learning*, which states that a behavior that results in a pleasant event tends to be repeated. Likewise a behavior that results in an unpleasant event tends not to be repeated. It is this theory on

It is an absolute necessity for the Neo owner to be in complete control when his giant dog is on lead.

HOUSE-TRAINING TIP

Most of all, be consistent. Always take your dog to the same location, always use the same command and always have the dog on lead when he is in his relief area, unless a fenced-in yard is available.

By following the Success Method, your puppy will be completely housebroken by the time his muscle and brain development reach maturity. Keep in mind that small breeds usually mature faster than large breeds, but all puppies should be trained by six months of age.

Use only the strongest collars and leads for your Neo. These Neos are already massive, and they are not yet full grown! Venere della Grotta Azzurra (left) is seven months old, and Vera della Grotta Azzurra is six months old. Owned by La Tutela Kennels.

which training methods are based today. For example, if you manipulate a dog to perform a specific behavior and reward

KEEP SMILING

Never train your dog, puppy or adult, when you are angry or in a sour mood. Dogs are very sensitive to human feelings, especially anger, and if your dog senses that you are angry or upset, he will connect your anger with his training and learn to resent or fear his training sessions.

him for doing it, he is likely to do it again because he enjoyed the end result.

Occasionally, punishment, a penalty inflicted for an offense, is necessary. The best type of punishment often comes from an outside source. For example, a child is told not to touch the stove because he may get burned. He disobeys and touches the stove. In doing so, he receives a burn. From that time on, he respects the heat of the stove and avoids contact with it. Therefore, a behavior that results in an unpleasant event tends not to be repeated.

A good example of a dog learning the hard way is the dog who chases the house cat. He is told many times to leave the cat alone, yet he persists in teasing the cat. Then, one day he begins chasing the cat but the cat turns and swipes a claw across the dog's face, leaving him with a painful gash on his nose. The final result is that the dog stops chasing the cat.

TRAINING EQUIPMENT

COLLAR AND LEAD
For a Neapolitan Mastiff, the collar and lead that you use for training must be one with which you are easily able to work, not too heavy for the dog and perfectly safe. If your dog pulls mightily on the leash, you may require a chain choker collar.

TREATS
Have a bag of treats on hand. Something nutritious and easy to swallow works best. Use a soft treat, a chunk of cheese or a piece of cooked chicken rather than a dry biscuit. By the time the dog gets done chewing a dry treat, he will forget why he is being rewarded in the first place! Using food rewards will not teach a dog to beg at the table—the only way to teach a dog to beg at the table is to give him food from the table. In

PRACTICE MAKES PERFECT!

- Have training lessons with your dog every day in several short segments—three to five times a day for a few minutes at a time is ideal.
- Do not have long practice sessions. The dog will become easily bored.

- Never practice when you are tired, ill, worried or in an otherwise negative mood. This will transmit to the dog and may have an adverse effect on his performance.

Think fun, short and above all *positive!* End each session on a high note, rather than a failed exercise, and make sure to give a lot of praise. Enjoy the training and help your dog enjoy it, too.

If your Neo responds to food like these two "chow-hounds," you will probably have an easy time training your dog by using treats as rewards.

training, rewarding the dog with a food treat will help him associate praise and the treats with learning new behaviors that obviously please his owner.

TRAINING BEGINS: ASK THE DOG A QUESTION

In order to teach your dog anything, you must first get his attention. After all, he cannot learn anything if he is looking away from you with his mind on something else.

To get his attention, ask him, "School?" and immediately walk over to him and give him a treat as you tell him "Good dog." Wait a minute or two and repeat the routine, this time with a treat in your hand as you approach within a foot of the dog. Do not go directly to him, but stop about a foot short of him and hold out the treat as you ask, "School?" He will see you approaching with a treat in your hand and most likely begin walking toward you. As you meet, give him the treat and praise again.

The third time, ask the question, have a treat in your hand and walk only a short distance toward the dog so that he must walk almost all the way to you. As he reaches you, give him the treat and praise again.

By this time, the dog will probably be getting the idea that if he pays attention to you, especially when you ask that question, it will pay off in treats and fun activities for him. In other words, he learns that "school" means doing fun things with you that result in treats and positive attention for him.

Remember that the dog does not understand your verbal language, he only recognizes sounds. Your question translates to a series of sounds for him, and those sounds become the signal to go to you and pay attention; if he does, he will get to interact with you plus receive treats and praise.

THE BASIC COMMANDS

TEACHING SIT

Now that you have the dog's attention, attach his lead and hold it in your left hand and a food treat in your right. Place your food hand at the dog's nose and let him lick the treat but not take it from you. Say "Sit" and slowly raise your food hand from in front of the dog's nose up over his head so that he is looking at the ceiling. As he bends his head upward, he will have to bend his knees to maintain his balance. As he bends his knees, he will assume a sit position. At that point, release the food treat and praise lavishly with comments

When introducing the sit command, you may have to physically guide your dog into the correct position for the first few tries.

Every Neo must be taught to sit upon command. This is one of the most basic commands.

such as "Good dog! Good sit!" Remember to always praise enthusiastically, because dogs relish verbal praise from their owners and feel so proud of themselves whenever they accomplish a behavior.

You will not use food forever in getting the dog to obey your commands. Food is only used to teach new behaviors, and once the dog knows what you want when you give a specific command, you will wean him off the food treats but still maintain the verbal

95

A young Neo demonstrates how well he has learned his first lesson...sit.

you do not. Dogs perceive the down position as a submissive one, therefore teaching the down exercise using a forceful method can sometimes make the dog develop such a fear of the down that he either runs away when you say "Down" or he attempts to snap at the person who tries to force him down.

Have the dog sit close alongside your left leg, facing in the same direction as you are. Hold the lead in your left hand and a food treat in your right. Now place your left hand lightly on the top of the dog's shoulders where they meet above the spinal cord. Do not push down on the dog's shoulders; simply rest your left hand there so you can guide the dog to lie down

LANGUAGE BARRIER

Dogs do not understand our language and have to rely on tone of voice more than just works or sound. They can be trained to react to a certain sound, at a certain volume. If you say "No, Oliver" in a very soft, pleasant voice, it will not have the same meaning as "No, Oliver!!" when you shout it as loud as you can. You should never use the dog's name during a reprimand, just the command "No! "

You never want the dog to associate his name with a negative experience or reprimand.

praise. After all, you will always have your voice with you, and there will be many times when you have no food rewards but expect the dog to obey.

TEACHING DOWN

Teaching the down exercise is easy when you understand how the dog perceives the down position, and it is very difficult when close to your left leg rather than to swing away from your side when he drops.

Now place the food hand at the dog's nose, say "Down" very softly (almost a whisper), and slowly lower the food hand to the dog's front feet. When the food hand reaches the floor, begin moving it forward along the floor in front of the dog. Keep talking softly to the dog, saying things like, "Do you want this treat? You can do this, good dog." Your reassuring tone of voice will help calm the dog as he tries to follow the food hand in order to get the treat.

When the dog's elbows touch the floor, release the food and praise softly. Try to get the dog to maintain that down position for several seconds before you let him sit up again. The goal here is to get the dog to settle down and not feel threatened in the down position.

TEACHING STAY

It is easy to teach the dog to stay in either a sit or a down position. Again, we use food and praise during the teaching process as we help the dog to understand exactly what it is that we are expecting him to do.

To teach the sit/stay, start with the dog sitting on your left side as before and hold the lead in your left hand. Have a food treat in your right hand and

DOUBLE JEOPARDY

A dog in jeopardy never lies down. He stays alert on his feet because instinct tells him that he may have to run away or fight for his survival. Therefore, if a dog feels threatened or anxious, he will not lie down. Consequently, it is important to keep the dog calm and relaxed as he learns the down exercise.

Teaching down may be difficult at first. Your Neo may need some extra coaxing to assume the position, which is viewed by dogs as a submissive posture.

Teach your Neo to stay. It is not a difficult exercise, and it can be taught with a combination of voice commands and hand signals.

place your food hand at the dog's nose. Say "Stay" and step out on your right foot to stand directly in front of the dog, toe to toe, as he licks and nibbles the treat. Be sure to keep his head facing upward to maintain the sit position. Count to five and then swing around to stand next to the dog again with him on your left. As soon as you get back to the original position, release the food and praise lavishly.

To teach the down/stay, do the down as previously described. As soon as the dog lies down, say "Stay" and step out on your right foot just as you did in the sit/stay. Count to five and then return to stand beside the dog with him on

FETCH!

Play fetching games with your puppy in an enclosed area where he can retrieve his toy and bring it

back to you. Always use a toy or object designated just for this purpose. Never use a shoe, sock or other item he may later confuse with those in your closet or underneath your chair.

your left side. Release the treat and praise as always.

Within a week or ten days, you can begin to add a bit of distance between you and your dog when you leave him. When you do, use your left hand open with the palm facing the dog as a stay signal, much the same as the hand signal a police officer uses to stop traffic at an intersection. Hold the food treat in your right hand as before, but this time the food is not touching the dog's nose. He will watch the food hand and quickly learn that he is going to get that treat as soon as you return to his side.

Naptimes between lessons is every Neo's favorite part of school.

When you can stand 1 yard away from your dog for 30 seconds, you can then begin building time and distance in both stays. Eventually, the dog can be expected to remain in the stay position for prolonged periods of time until you return to him or call him to you. Always praise lavishly when he stays.

"COME" . . . BACK

Never call your dog to come to you for a correction or scold him when he reaches you. That is the quickest way to turn a "Come" command into "Go away fast!" Dogs think only in the present tense, and your dog will connect the scolding with coming to you, not with the misbehavior of a few moments earlier.

TEACHING COME

If you make teaching "come" a fun experience, you should never have a student that does not love the game or that fails to come when called. The secret, it seems, is never to teach the word "come."

At times when an owner most wants his dog to come when called, the owner is likely upset or anxious and he allows these feelings to come through in the tone of his voice when he calls his dog. Hearing that desperation in his owner's voice, the dog fears the results of going to him and therefore either disobeys outright or runs in the opposite direction. The secret, therefore, is to teach the dog a game and, when you want him to come to you, simply play the

99

Neapolitan Mastiff

You certainly should teach your Neo to come when called. Greet your pup with praise and petting, and he should always want to run to you.

game. It is practically a no-fail solution!

To begin, have several members of your family take a few food treats and each go into a different room in the house. Take turns calling the dog, and each person should celebrate the dog's finding him with a treat and lots of happy praise. When a person calls the dog, he is actually inviting the dog to find him and get a treat as a reward for "winning."

A few turns of the "Where are you?" game and the dog will figure out that everyone is playing the game and that each person has a big celebration awaiting his success at locating them. Once he learns to love the game, simply calling out "Where are you?" will bring him running from wherever he is when he hears that all-important question.

The come command is recognized as one of the most important things to teach a dog, but there are trainers who work with thousands of dogs and never teach

the actual word "come." Yet these dogs will race to respond to a person who uses the dog's name followed by "Where are you?" For example, a woman has a 12-year-old companion dog who went blind, but who never fails to locate her owner when asked, "Where are you?"

Children particularly love to play this game with their dogs. Children can hide in smaller places like a shower or bathtub, behind a bed or under a table. The dog needs to work a little bit harder to find these hiding places, but when he does he loves to celebrate with a treat and a tussle with a favorite youngster.

TEACHING HEEL

Heeling means that the dog walks beside the owner without pulling. It takes time and patience on the owner's part to succeed at teaching the dog that he (the owner) will not proceed

---

"WHERE ARE YOU?"

When calling the dog, do not say "Come." Say things like, "Rover, where are you? See if you can find me! I have a biscuit for you!" Keep up a constant line of chatter with coaxing sounds and frequent questions such as, "Where are you?" The dog will learn to follow the sound of your voice to locate you and receive his reward.

HEELING WELL

Teach your dog to heel in an enclosed area. Once you think the dog will obey reliably and you want to attempt advanced obedience exercises such as off-lead heeling, test him in a fenced-in area so he cannot run away.

With a dog as large as a Neo, he must be taught to walk alongside you without pulling or stopping. The heel exercise is required; the dog must learn to walk at your pace and stop when you stop.

unless the dog is walking calmly beside him. Pulling out ahead on the lead is definitely not acceptable.

Begin with holding the lead in your left hand as the dog sits beside your left leg. Move the loop end of the lead to your right hand but keep your left hand short on the lead so it keeps the dog in close next to you.

Say "Heel" and step forward on your left foot. Keep the dog close to you and take three steps. Stop and have the dog sit next to you in what we now call the heel position. Praise verbally, but do not touch the dog. Hesitate a moment and begin again with "Heel," taking three steps and stopping, at which point the dog is told to sit again.

Your goal here is to have the dog walk those three steps without pulling on the lead. When he will walk calmly beside you for three steps without pulling, increase the number of steps you take to five. When he will walk politely beside you while you take five steps, you can increase the length of your walk to ten steps. Keep increasing the length of your stroll until the dog will walk quietly beside you without pulling as long as you want him to heel. When you stop heeling, indicate to the dog that the exercise is over by verbally praising as you pet him and say "OK, good dog." The "OK" is used as a release word, meaning that the exercise is finished and the dog is free to relax.

If you are dealing with a dog who insists on pulling you around, simply "put on your brakes" and stand your ground until the dog realizes that the two of you are not going anywhere until he is beside you and moving at your pace, not his. It may take some time just standing there to convince the dog that you are the leader and you will be the one to decide on the direction and speed of your travel.

Each time the dog looks up at you or slows down to give a slack lead between the two of you, quietly praise him and say, "Good heel. Good dog." Eventually, the dog will begin to respond and within a few days he will be walking politely beside you without pulling on the lead. At first,

the training sessions should be kept short and very positive; soon the dog will be able to walk nicely with you for increasingly longer distances. Remember also to give the dog free time and the opportunity to run and play when you are done with heel practice.

WEANING OFF FOOD IN TRAINING

Food is used in training new behaviors. Once the dog understands what behavior goes with a specific command, it is time to start weaning him off the food treats. At first, give a treat after each exercise. Then, start to give a treat only after every other exercise. Mix up the times when you offer a food reward and the times when you only offer praise so that the dog will never know when he is going to receive both food and praise and when he is going to receive only praise. This is called a variable ratio reward system and it proves successful because there is always the chance that the owner will produce a treat, so the dog never stops trying for that reward. No matter what, *always* give verbal praise.

OBEDIENCE CLASSES

It is a good idea to enroll in an obedience class if one is available in your area. If yours is a show dog, handling classes would be more appropriate. Many areas have dog clubs that offer basic obedi-

TUG OF WALK?

If you begin teaching the heel by taking long walks and letting the dog pull you along, he misinterprets this action as an acceptable form of taking a walk. When you pull back on the lead to counteract his pulling, he reads that tug as a signal to pull even harder!

ence training as well as preparatory classes for obedience competition. There are also local dog trainers who offer similar classes.

At obedience trials, dogs can earn titles at various levels of competition. The beginning levels of competition include basic behaviors such as sit, down, heel, etc. The more advanced levels of competition include jumping, retrieving, scent discrimination and signal work. The advanced levels require a dog and owner to put a lot of time and effort into their training and the titles that can be earned at these levels of competition are very prestigious.

OTHER ACTIVITIES FOR LIFE
Whether a dog is trained in the structured environment of a class or alone with his owner at home, there are many activities that can bring fun and rewards to both owner and dog once they have mastered basic control.

Teaching the dog to help out around the home, in the yard or on the farm provides great satisfaction to both dog and owner. In addition, the dog's help makes life a little easier for his owner and raises his stature as a valued companion to his family. It helps give the dog a purpose by occupying his

OBEDIENCE SCHOOL

A basic obedience beginner's class usually lasts for six to eight weeks. Dog and owner attend an hour-long lesson once a week and practice for a few minutes, several times a day, each day at home. If done properly, the whole procedure will result in a well-mannered dog and an owner who delights in living with a pet that is eager to please and enjoys doing things with his owner.

mind and providing an outlet for his energy.

Backpacking is an exciting and healthy activity that the dog can be taught without assistance from more than his owner. The exercise of walking and climbing is good for man and dog alike, and the bond that they develop together is priceless.

Dog ownership opens up a world of new experiences for dog and owner. Contact a local kennel club to learn about the different activities in which you and your Neo can become involved.

Dogs suffer from many of the same physical illnesses as people. They might even share many of the same psychological

even though dogs don't have symptoms, which are verbal descriptions of the patient's feelings: dogs have *clinical signs*.

Take your Neo puppy to the local vet soon after you buy him to have his overall health assessed.

Since dogs can't speak, we have to look for clinical signs...but we still use the term *symptoms* in this book.

As a general rule, medicine is practiced. That term is not arbitrary. Medicine is a constantly changing art as we learn

problems. Since people usually know more about human diseases than canine maladies, many of the terms used in this chapter will be familiar but not necessarily those used by veterinarians. We will use the term *x-ray*, instead of the more acceptable term *radiograph*. We will also use the familiar term *symptoms*

more and more about genetics, electronic aids (like CAT scans and MRIs) and daily laboratory advances. There are many dog maladies, like canine hip dysplasia, which are not universally treated in the same manner. Some veterinarians opt for surgery more often than others do.

SELECTING A VETERINARIAN

Your selection of a veterinarian should be based not only upon personality and ability with large dogs but also upon his convenience to your home. You want a vet who is close because you might have emergencies or need to make multiple visits for treatments. You want a vet who has services that you might require such as tattooing and grooming facilities, as well as sophisticated pet supplies and a good reputation for ability and responsiveness. There is nothing more frustrating than having to wait a day or more to get a response from your veterinarian.

All veterinarians are licensed and their diplomas and/or certificates should be displayed in their waiting rooms. There are, however, many veterinary specialties that usually require further studies and internships. There are specialists in heart problems (veterinary cardiologists), skin problems (veterinary dermatologists), teeth and gum problems (veterinary dentists), eye problems (veterinary ophthalmologists), x-rays (veterinary radiologists) and surgeons who have specialities in bones, muscles or other organs. Most veterinarians do routine surgery such as neutering, stitching up wounds and docking tails for those breeds in which such is

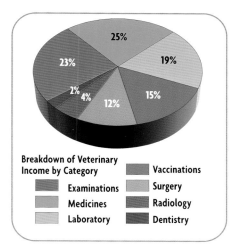

Breakdown of Veterinary Income by Category

- Vaccinations
- Examinations
- Surgery
- Medicines
- Radiology
- Laboratory
- Dentistry

A typical vet's income categorized according to services performed. This survey dealt with small-animal (pet) practices.

required for show purposes. When the problem affecting your dog is serious, it is not unusual or impudent to get another medical opinion, although it's courteous to advise the vets concerned about this. You might also want to compare costs among several veterinarians. Sophisticated health care and veterinary services can be very costly. Don't be bashful about discussing these costs with your veterinarian or his staff. Important decisions are often based upon financial considerations.

PREVENTATIVE MEDICINE

It is much easier, less costly and more effective to practice preventative medicine than to fight bouts of illness and disease. Properly bred puppies come from parents that were selected based upon their genetic-disease

Internal Organs with Skeletal Structure

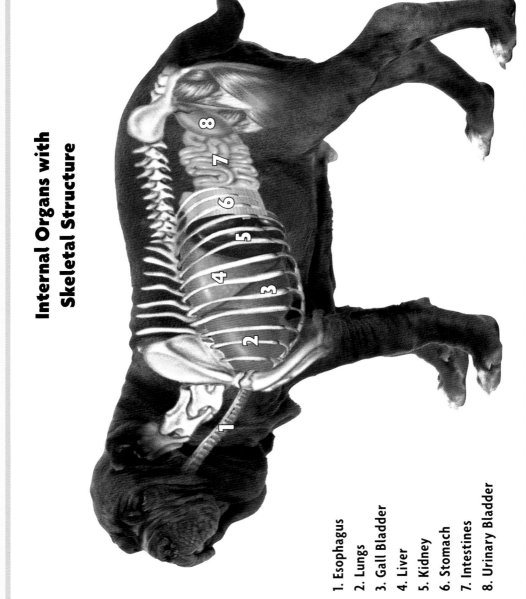

1. Esophagus
2. Lungs
3. Gall Bladder
4. Liver
5. Kidney
6. Stomach
7. Intestines
8. Urinary Bladder

profile. Their dam should have been vaccinated, free of all internal and external parasites, and properly nourished. For these reasons, a visit to the veterinarian who cared for the dam is recommended. The dam can pass on disease resistance to her puppies, which can last for eight to ten weeks. She can also pass on parasites and many infections. That's why you should learn as much about the dam's health as possible.

WEANING TO FIVE MONTHS OLD
Puppies should be weaned by the time they are about two months old. A puppy that remains for at least eight weeks with his mother and littermates usually adapts better to other dogs and people later in his life.

Some new owners have their puppy examined by a veterinarian immediately, which is a good idea. Vaccination programs usually begin when the puppy is very young. The puppy will have his teeth examined and have his skeletal conformation and general health checked prior to certification by the veterinarian. Puppies in certain breeds have problems with their kneecaps, cataracts and other eye problems, heart murmurs and undescended testicles. They may also have personality problems and your veterinarian might have training in temperament evaluation.

HOW TO PREVENT BLOAT

Research has confirmed that the structure of deep-chested breeds contributes to their predisposition to bloat. Nevertheless, there are several precautions that you can take to reduce the risk of this condition:

- Feed your dog twice daily rather than offer one big meal.
- Do not exercise your dog for at least one hour before and two hours after he has eaten.
- Make certain that your dog is calm and not overly excited while he is eating. It has been proven that nervous or overly excited dogs are more prone to develop bloat.
- Add a small portion of moist meat product to his dry food ration.
- Serve his meals in an elevated bowl stand, which avoids the dog's craning his neck while eating.
- To prevent your dog from gobbling his food too quickly, and thereby swallowing air, put some large (unswallowable) toys into his bowl so that he will have to eat around them to get his food.

VACCINATION SCHEDULING
Most vaccinations are given by injection and should only be done by a veterinarian. Both you and he should keep a record of the date of the injection, the identification of the vaccine and the amount given. Some vets give a first vaccination at eight weeks, but most dog breeders

107

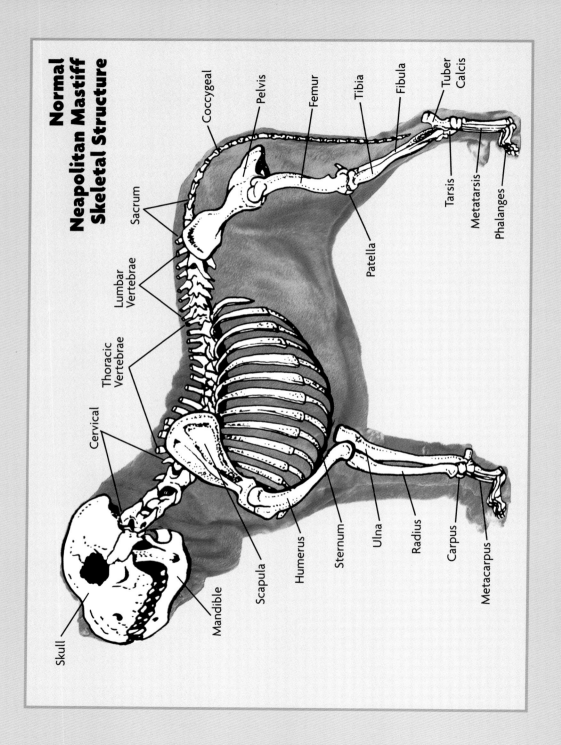

Normal
Neapolitan Mastiff
Skeletal Structure

Coccygeal

Pelvis

Femur

Tibia

Fibula

Tuber
Calcis

Tarsis

Metatarsis

Phalanges

Patella

Sacrum

Lumbar
Vertebrae

Thoracic
Vertebrae

Cervical

Metacarpus

Carpus

Radius

Ulna

Sternum

Humerus

Scapula

Mandible

Skull

prefer the course not to commence until about ten weeks because of negating any antibodies passed on by the dam. The vaccination scheduling is usually based on a 15-day cycle. You must take your vet's advice as to when to vaccinate as this may differ according to the vaccine used. Most vaccinations immunize your puppy against viruses.

The usual vaccines contain immunizing doses of several different viruses such as distemper, parvovirus, parainfluenza and hepatitis. There are other vaccines available when the puppy is at risk. You should rely upon professional advice. This is especially true for the booster-shot program. Most vaccination programs require a booster when the puppy is a year old and once a year thereafter. In some cases, circumstances may require more frequent immunizations.

Canine cough, more formally known as tracheobronchitis, is treated with a vaccine that is sprayed into the dog's nostrils. Canine cough is usually included in routine vaccination, but this is often not so effective as for other major diseases.

FIVE MONTHS TO ONE YEAR OF AGE
Unless you intend to breed or show your dog, neutering the puppy at six months of age is recommended. Discuss this with

BE CAREFUL WHERE YOU WALK YOUR DOG

Dogs who have been exposed to lawns sprayed with herbicides have double and triple the rate of malignant lymphoma. Suburban dogs are

especially at risk, as they are exposed to manicured lawns and gardens. Dogs perspire and absorb through their footpads. Be careful where your dog walks and always avoid any area that appears yellowed from chemical overspray. These chemicals are not good for you, either!

your veterinarian; most professionals advise neutering the puppy. Neutering has proven to be extremely beneficial to both male and female dogs. Besides eliminating the possibility of pregnancy, it inhibits (but does not prevent) breast cancer in bitches and prostate cancer in

HEALTH AND VACCINATION SCHEDULE

Age in Weeks:	6TH	8TH	10TH	12TH	14TH	16TH	20-24TH	1 YR
Worm Control	✔	✔	✔	✔	✔	✔	✔	
Neutering								✔
Heartworm		✔		✔		✔	✔	
Parvovirus	✔		✔		✔		✔	✔
Distemper		✔		✔		✔		✔
Hepatitis		✔		✔		✔		✔
Leptospirosis								✔
Parainfluenza	✔		✔		✔			✔
Dental Examination		✔					✔	✔
Complete Physical		✔					✔	✔
Coronavirus				✔			✔	✔
Canine Cough	✔							
Hip Dysplasia								✔
Rabies							✔	

Vaccinations are not instantly effective. It takes about two weeks for the dog's immunization system to develop antibodies. Most vaccinations require annual booster shots. Your veterinarian should guide you in this regard.

male dogs. It is very rare to diagnose breast cancer in a female dog who was spayed at or before about nine months of age before her first heat.

Your veterinarian should provide your puppy with a thorough dental evaluation at six months of age, ascertaining whether all of the permanent teeth have erupted properly. A home dental-care regimen should be initiated at six months, including brushing weekly and providing good dental devices (such as nylon bones). Regular dental care promotes healthy teeth, fresh breath and a longer life.

ONE TO SEVEN YEARS
Once a year, your grown dog should visit the vet for an examination and vaccination boosters. Some vets recommend blood tests, thyroid level check and dental evaluation to accompany these annual visits. A thorough clinical evaluation by the vet can provide critical background information for your dog. Blood tests are often performed at one year of age, and dental examinations around the third or fourth birthday. In the long run, quality preventative care for your pet can save money, teeth and lives.

SKIN PROBLEMS IN NEAPOLITAN MASTIFFS

Veterinarians are consulted by dog owners for skin problems more than any other group of diseases or maladies. Dogs' skin is almost as sensitive as human skin and both suffer from almost the same ailments (though the occurrence of acne in dogs is rare!). For this reason, veterinary dermatology has developed into a specialty practiced by many veterinarians.

Since many skin problems have visual symptoms that are almost identical, it requires the skill of an experienced veterinary dermatologist to identify and cure many of the more severe skin disorders. Pet shops sell many treatments for skin problems but most of the treatments are directed at symptoms and not the underlying problem(s). If your dog is suffering from a skin disorder, you should seek professional assistance as quickly as possible. As with all diseases, the earlier a problem is identified and treated, the more successful is the cure.

DISEASE REFERENCE CHART

	What is it?	What causes it?	Symptoms
Leptospirosis	Severe disease that affects the internal organs; can be spread to people.	A bacterium, which is often carried by rodents, that enters through mucous membranes and spreads quickly throughout the body.	Range from fever, vomiting and loss of appetite in less severe cases to shock, irreversible kidney damage and possibly death in most severe cases.
Rabies	Potentially deadly virus that infects warm-blooded mammals. Not seen in United Kingdom.	Bite from a carrier of the virus, mainly wild animals.	1st stage: dog exhibits change in behavior, fear. 2nd stage: dog's behavior becomes more aggressive. 3rd stage: loss of coordination, trouble with bodily functions.
Parvovirus	Highly contagious virus, potentially deadly.	Ingestion of the virus, which is usually spread through the faeces of infected dogs.	Most common: severe diarrhea. Also vomiting, fatigue, lack of appetite.
Canine cough	Contagious respiratory infection.	Combination of types of bacteria and virus. Most common: *Bordetella bronchiseptica* bacteria and parainfluenza virus.	Chronic cough.
Distemper	Disease primarily affecting respiratory and nervous system.	Virus that is related to the human measles virus.	Mild symptoms such as fever, lack of appetite and mucus secretion progress to evidence of brain damage, "hard pad."
Hepatitis	Virus primarily affecting the liver.	Canine adenovirus type I (CAV-1). Enters system when dog breathes in particles.	Lesser symptoms include listlessness, diarrhea, vomiting. More severe symptoms include "blue-eye" (clumps of virus in eye).
Coronavirus	Virus resulting in digestive problems.	Virus is spread through infected dog's feces.	Stomach upset evidenced by lack of appetite, vomiting, diarrhea.

HEREDITARY SKIN DISORDERS

Veterinary dermatologists are currently researching a number of skin disorders that are believed to have a hereditary basis. These inherited diseases are transmitted by both parents, who appear (phenotypically) normal but have a recessive gene for the disease, meaning that they carry, but are not affected by, the disease. These diseases pose serious problems to breeders because in some instances there are no methods of identifying carriers. Often the secondary diseases associated with these skin conditions are even more debilitating than the skin disorders themselves, including cancers and respiratory problems.

Among the hereditary skin disorders, for which the mode of inheritance is known, are acrodermatitis, cutaneous asthenia (Ehlers-Danlos syndrome), sebaceous adenitis, cyclic hematopoiesis, dermatomyositis, IgA deficiency, color dilution alopecia and nodular dermatofibrosis. Some of these disorders are limited to one or two breeds, while others affect a large number of breeds. All inherited diseases must be diagnosed and treated by a veterinary specialist.

PARASITE BITES

Many of us are allergic to insect bites. The bites itch, erupt and may even become infected. Dogs have the same reaction to fleas, ticks and/or mites. When an insect lands on you, you have the chance to whisk it away with your hand. Unfortunately, when your dog is bitten by a flea, tick or mite, he can only scratch it away or bite it. By the time the dog has been bitten, the parasite has done some of its damage. It may also have laid eggs to cause further problems in the near future. The itching from parasite bites is probably due to the saliva injected into the site when the parasite sucks the dog's blood.

AUTO-IMMUNE SKIN CONDITIONS

Auto-immune skin conditions are commonly referred to as being allergic to yourself, while allergies are usually inflammatory reactions to an outside stimulus. Auto-immune diseases cause serious damage to the tissues that are involved.

The best known auto-immune disease is lupus, which

CLEAR WATER

Never allow your dog to swim in polluted water or public areas where water quality can be suspect. Even perfectly clear water can harbor parasites, many of which can cause serious to fatal illnesses in canines. Areas inhabited by waterfowl and other wildlife are especially dangerous.

affects people as well as dogs. The symptoms are variable and may affect the kidneys, bones, blood chemistry and skin. It can be fatal to both dogs and humans, though it is not thought to be transmissible. It is usually successfully treated with cortisone, prednisone or similar corticosteroid, but extensive use of these drugs can have harmful side effects.

ACRAL LICK DERMATITIS

Neapolitan Mastiffs and many other dogs have a very poorly understood syndrome called acral lick. The manifestation of the problem is the dog's tireless attack at a specific area of the body, almost always the legs. They lick so intensively that they remove the hair and skin leaving an ugly, large wound. There is no absolute cure, but corticosteroids are the most common treatment.

AIRBORNE ALLERGIES

Just as humans have hay fever, rose fever and other fevers from which they suffer during the pollinating season, many dogs suffer from the same allergies. When the pollen count is high your dog might suffer, but don't expect him to sneeze and have a runny nose as a human would. Dogs react to pollen allergies the same way they react to fleas—they scratch and bite themselves.

PET ADVANTAGES

If you do not intend to show or breed your new puppy, your veterinarian will probably recommend that you spay your female or neuter your male. Some people believe neutering leads to weight gain, but if you feed and exercise your dog properly, this is easily avoided. Spaying or neutering can actually have many positive outcomes, such as:

- training becomes easier, as the dog focuses less on the urge to mate and more on you!
- females are protected from unplanned pregnancy as well as ovarian and uterine cancers.
- males are guarded from testicular tumors and have a reduced risk of developing prostate cancer.

Talk to your vet regarding the right age to spay/neuter and other aspects of the procedure.

Dogs, like humans, can be tested for allergens. Discuss the testing with your veterinary dermatologist.

FOOD PROBLEMS

FOOD ALLERGIES

Dogs are allergic to many foods that are best-sellers and highly recommended by breeders and veterinarians. Changing the brand of food that you buy may not eliminate the problem if the

DENTAL HEALTH

A dental examination is in order when the dog is between six months and one year of age so that any permanent teeth that have erupted incorrectly can be corrected. It is important to begin a brushing routine, and remain

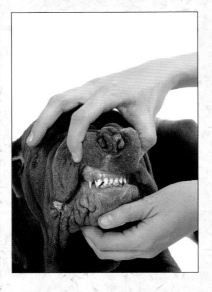

consistent with it throughout the dog's lifetime. Durable nylon and safe edible chews should be a part of your puppy's arsenal for good health, good teeth and pleasant breath. The vast majority of dogs three to four years old and older has diseases of the gums from lack of dental attention. Using the various types of dental chews can be very effective in controlling dental plaque.

Acral lick is a poorly understood behavior in which a dog, particularly of a large breed, constantly licks at a spot on his foreleg until the hair wears away and an open sore forms.

element to which the dog is allergic is contained in the new brand.

Recognizing a food allergy is difficult. Humans vomit or have rashes when they eat a food to which they are allergic. Dogs neither vomit nor (usually) develop a rash. They react in the same manner as they do to an airborne or flea allergy: they itch, scratch and bite. Thus making the diagnosis extremely difficult. While pollen allergies and parasite bites are usually seasonal, food allergies are year-round problems.

FOOD INTOLERANCE

Food intolerance is the inability of the dog to completely digest certain foods. For example, puppies that may have done very well on their mother's milk may not do well on cow's milk. The result of this food intolerance may be loose bowels, passing gas and stomach pains. These are the only obvious symptoms of food intolerance and that makes diagnosis difficult.

TTREATING FOOD PROBLEMS

It is possible to handle food allergies and food intolerance yourself. Put your dog on a diet that he has never had. Obviously if he has never eaten this new food he can't have been allergic or intolerant of it. Start with a single ingredient that is not in the dog's diet at the present time. Ingredients like chopped beef or chicken are common in dogs' diets, so try something more exotic like rabbit, pheasant or another source of protein. Keep the dog on this diet (with no additives) for a month. If the symptoms of food allergy or intolerance disappear, chances are your dog has a food allergy.

Don't think that the single ingredient cured the problem. You still must find a suitable diet and ascertain which ingredient in the old diet was objectionable. This is most easily done by adding ingredients to the new diet one at a time. Let the dog stay on the modified diet for a month before you add another ingredient. Eventually, you will determine the ingredient that caused the adverse reaction.

An alternative method is to carefully study the ingredients in the diet to which your dog is allergic or intolerant. Identify the main ingredient in this diet and eliminate the main ingredient by buying a different food that does not have that ingredient. Keep experimenting until the symptoms disappear after one month on the new diet.

CARETAKER OF TEETH

You are your dog's caretaker and his dentist. Vets warn that plaque and tartar buildup on the teeth will

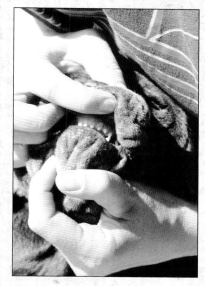

damage the gums and allow bacteria to enter the dog's bloodstream, causing serious damage to the animal's vital organs. Studies show that over 50% of dogs have some form of gum disease before age three. Daily or weekly tooth cleaning (with a brush or soft gauze pad wipes) can add to your dog's life.

First Aid at a Glance

Burns
Place the affected area under cool water; use ice if only a small area is burnt.

Bee Stings/Insect bites
Apply ice to relieve swelling; antihistamine dosed properly.

Animal bites
Clean any bleeding area; apply pressure until bleeding subsides; go to the vet.

Spider bites
Use cold compress and a pressurized pack to inhibit venom's spreading.

Antifreeze poisoning
Immediately induce vomiting by using hydrogen peroxide.

Fish hooks
Removal best handled by vet; hook must be cut in order to remove.

Snake bites
Pack ice around bite; contact vet quickly; identify snake for proper antivenin.

Car accident
Move dog from roadway with blanket; seek veterinary aid.

Shock
Calm the dog, keep him warm; seek immediate veterinary help.

Nosebleed
Apply cold compress to the nose; apply pressure to any visible abrasion.

Bleeding
Apply pressure above the area; treat wound by applying a cotton pack.

Heat stroke
Submerge dog in cold bath; cool down with fresh air and water; go to the vet.

Frostbite/Hypothermia
Warm the dog with a warm bath, electric blankets or hot-water bottles.

Abrasions
Clean the wound and wash out thoroughly with fresh water; apply antiseptic.

 Remember: an injured dog may attempt to bite a helping hand from fear and confusion. Always muzzle the dog before trying to offer assistance.

Number-One Killer Disease in Dogs: CANCER

In every age there is a word associated with a disease or plague that causes humans to shudder. In the 21st century, that word is 'cancer.' Just as cancer is the leading cause of death in humans, it claims nearly half the lives of dogs that die from a natural disease as well as half the dogs that die over the age of ten years.

Described as a genetic disease, cancer becomes a greater risk as the dog ages. Veterinary surgeons and dog owners have become increasingly aware of the threat of cancer to dogs. Statistics reveal that one dog in every five will develop cancer, the most common of which is skin cancer. Many cancers, including prostate, ovarian and breast cancer, can be avoided by spaying and neutering our dogs by the age of six months.

Early detection of cancer can save or extend your dog's life, so it is absolutely vital for owners to have their dogs examined by a qualified veterinary surgeon or oncologist immediately upon detection of any abnormality. Certain dietary guidelines have also proven to reduce the onset and spread of cancer. Foods based on fish rather than beef, due to the presence of Omega-3 fatty acids, are recommended. Other amino acids such as glutamine have significant benefits for canines, particularly those breeds that show a greater susceptibility to cancer.

Cancer management and treatments promise hope for future generations of canines. Since the disease is genetic, breeders should never breed a dog whose parents, grandparents and any related siblings have developed cancer. It is difficult to know whether to exclude an otherwise healthy dog from a breeding programme as the disease does not manifest itself until the dog's senior years.

RECOGNISE CANCER WARNING SIGNS

Since early detection can possibly rescue your dog from becoming a cancer statistic, it is essential for owners to recognise the possible signs and seek the assistance of a qualified professional.

- Abnormal bumps or lumps that continue to grow
- Bleeding or discharge from any body cavity
- Persistent stiffness or lameness
- Recurrent sores or sores that do not heal
- Inappetence
- Breathing difficulties
- Weight loss
- Bad breath or odours
- General malaise and fatigue
- Eating and swallowing problems
- Difficulty urinating and defecating

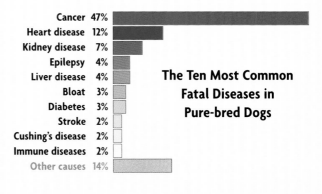

Cancer	47%
Heart disease	12%
Kidney disease	7%
Epilepsy	4%
Liver disease	4%
Bloat	3%
Diabetes	3%
Stroke	2%
Cushing's disease	2%
Immune diseases	2%
Other causes	14%

The Ten Most Common Fatal Diseases in Pure-bred Dogs

A male dog flea, *Ctenocephalides canis.*

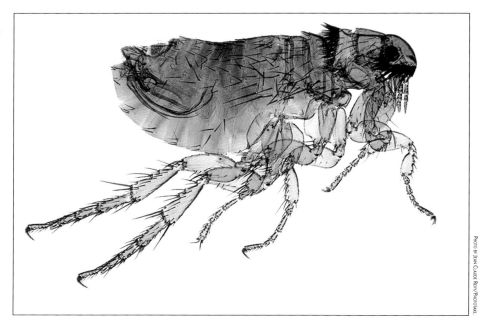

EXTERNAL PARASITES

FLEAS

Of all the problems to which dogs are prone, none is more well known and frustrating than fleas. Flea infestation is relatively simple to cure but difficult to prevent. Parasites that are harbored inside the body are a bit more difficult to eradicate but they are easier to control.

To control flea infestation, you have to understand the flea's life cycle. Fleas are often thought of as a summertime problem, but centrally heated homes have changed the patterns and fleas can be found at any time of the year. The most effective method of flea control is a two-stage approach: one stage to kill the adult fleas, and the other to control the development of pre-adult fleas. Unfortunately, no single active ingredient is effective against all stages of the life cycle.

FLEA KILLER CAUTION— "POISON"

Flea-killers are poisonous. You should not spray these toxic chemicals on areas of a dog's body that he licks, including his genitals and his face. Flea killers taken internally are a better answer, but check with your vet in case internal therapy is not advised for your dog.

LIFE CYCLE STAGES

During its life, a flea will pass through four life stages: egg, larva, pupa or nymph and adult. The adult stage is the most visible and irritating stage of the flea life cycle, and this is why the majority of flea-control products concentrate on this stage. The fact is that adult fleas account for only 1% of the total flea population, and the other 99% exist in pre-adult stages, i.e. eggs, larvae and nymphs. The pre-adult stages are barely visible to the naked eye.

THE LIFE CYCLE OF THE FLEA

Eggs are laid on the dog, usually in quantities of about 20 or 30, several times a day. The adult female flea must have a blood meal before each egg-laying session. When first laid, the eggs will cling to the dog's hair, as the eggs are still moist. However, they will quickly dry out and fall from the dog, especially if the dog moves around or scratches. Many eggs will fall off in the dog's favorite area or an area in which he spends a lot of time, such as his bed.

Once the eggs fall from the dog onto the carpet or furniture, they will hatch into larvae. This takes from one to ten days. Larvae are not particularly mobile and will usually travel only a few inches from where they hatch. However, they do have a tendency to move away from bright light and heavy

EN GARDE:
CATCHING FLEAS OFF GUARD!
Consider the following ways to arm yourself against fleas:
- Add a small amount of pennyroyal or eucalyptus oil to your dog's bath. These natural remedies repel fleas.
- Supplement your dog's food with fresh garlic (minced or grated) and an hearty amount of brewer's yeast, both of which ward off fleas.
- Use a flea comb on your dog daily. Submerge fleas in a cup of bleach to kill them quickly.
- Confine the dog to only a few rooms to limit the spread of fleas in the home.
- Vacuum daily...and get all of the crevices! Dispose of the bag every few days until the problem is under control.
- Wash your dog's bedding daily. Cover cushions where your dog sleeps with towels, and wash the towels often.

traffic—under furniture and behind doors are common places to find high quantities of flea larvae.

The flea larvae feed on dead organic matter, including adult flea feces, until they are ready to change into adult fleas. Fleas will usually remain as larvae for around seven days. After this period, the larvae will pupate into protective pupae. While inside the pupae, the larvae will undergo

Fleas have been measured as being able to jump 300,000 times and can jump 150 times their length in any direction, including straight up.

metamorphosis and change into adult fleas. This can take as little time as a few days, but the adult fleas can remain inside the pupae waiting to hatch for up to two years. The pupae are signaled to hatch by certain stimuli, such as physical pressure—the pupae's being stepped on, heat from an animal's lying on the pupae or increased carbon-dioxide levels and vibrations—indicating that a suitable host is available.

Once hatched, the adult flea must feed within a few days. Once the adult flea finds a host, it will not leave voluntarily. It only becomes dislodged by grooming or the host animal's scratching.

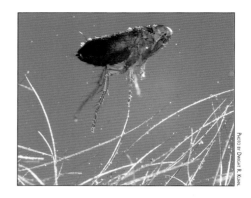

The adult flea will remain on the host for the duration of its life unless forcibly removed.

TREATING THE ENVIRONMENT AND THE DOG

Treating fleas should be a two-pronged attack. First, the environment needs to be treated; this includes carpets and furniture, especially the dog's bedding and areas underneath furniture. The environment should be treated with a household spray containing an Insect Growth Regulator (IGR) and an insecticide to kill the adult fleas. Most IGRs are effective against eggs and larvae; they actually mimic the fleas' own hormones and stop the eggs and larvae from developing into adult fleas. There are currently no treatments available to attack the pupa stage of the life cycle, so the adult insecticide is used to kill the newly hatched adult fleas before they find a host. Most IGRs are active for many months, while

A scanning electron micrograph of a dog or cat flea, *Ctenocephalides*, magnified more than 100x. This image has been colorized for effect.

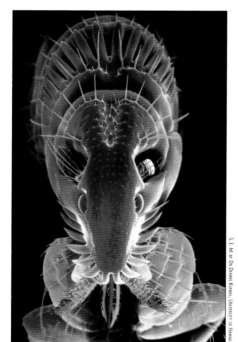

THE LIFE CYCLE OF THE FLEA

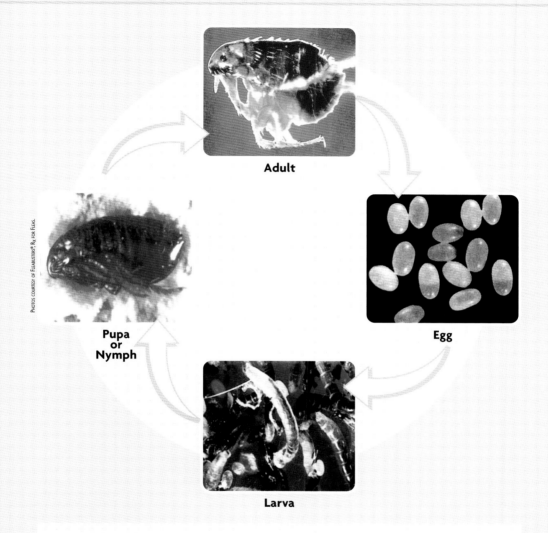

Adult

Egg

Larva

Pupa
or
Nymph

Fleas have been around for millions of years and have adapted to changing host animals. They are able to go through a complete life cycle in less than one month or they can extend their lives to almost two years by remaining as pupae or cocoons. They do not need blood or any other food for up to 20 months.

INSECT GROWTH REGULATOR (IGR)

Two types of products should be used when treating fleas—a product to treat the pet and a product to treat the home. Adult fleas represent less than 1% of the flea population. The pre-adult fleas (eggs, larvae and pupae) represent more than 99% of the flea population and are found in the environment; it is in the case of pre-adult fleas that products containing an Insect Growth Regulator (IGR) should be used in the home.

IGRs are a new class of compounds used to prevent the development of insects. They do not kill the insect outright, but instead use the insect's biology against it to stop it from completing its growth. Products that contain methoprene are the world's first and leading IGRs. Used to control fleas and other insects, this type of IGR will stop flea larvae from developing and protect the house for up to seven months.

The American dog tick, *Dermacentor variabilis*, is probably the most common tick found on dogs. Look at the strength in its eight legs! No wonder it's hard to detach them.

adult insecticides are only active for a few days.

When treating with a household spray, it is a good idea to vacuum before applying the product. This stimulates as many pupae as possible to hatch into adult fleas. The vacuum cleaner should also be treated with an insecticide to prevent the eggs and larvae that have been collected in the vacuum bag from hatching.

The second stage of treatment is to apply an adult insecticide to the dog. Traditionally, this would be in the form of a collar or a spray, but more recent innovations include digestible insecticides that poison the fleas when they ingest the dog's blood. Alternatively, there are drops that, when placed on the back of the dog's neck, spread throughout the dog's hair and skin to kill adult fleas.

TICKS

Though not as common as fleas, ticks are found all over the tropical and temperate world. They don't bite, like fleas; they harpoon. They dig their sharp proboscis (nose) into the dog's skin and drink the blood. Their

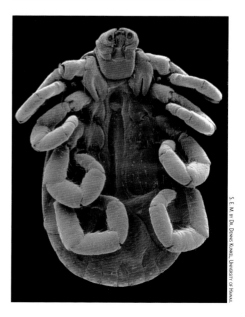

S.E.M. BY DR. DENNIS KUNKEL, UNIVERSITY OF HAWAII

only food and drink is dog's blood. Dogs can get Lyme disease, Rocky Mountain spotted fever, tick bite paralysis and many other diseases from ticks. They may live where fleas are found and they like to hide in cracks or seams in walls. They are controlled the same way fleas are controlled.

The American dog tick, *Dermacentor variabilis*, may well be the most common dog tick in many geographical areas, especially those areas where the climate is hot and humid. Most dog ticks have life expectancies of a week to six months, depending upon climatic conditions. They can neither jump nor fly, but they can crawl slowly and can range up to 16 feet to reach a sleeping or unsuspecting dog.

MITES

Just as fleas and ticks can be problematic for your dog, mites can also lead to an itchy nuisance. Microscopic in size, mites are related to ticks and generally take up permanent residence on their host animal— in this case, your dog! The term *mange* refers to any infestation caused by one of the mighty mites, of which there are six varieties that concern dog owners.

Demodex mites cause a condition known as demodicosis

DEER-TICK CROSSING

The great outdoors may be fun for your dog, but it also is an home to dangerous ticks. Deer ticks carry a bacterium known as *Borrelia burgdorferi* and are most active in the autumn and spring. When infections are caught early, penicillin and tetracycline are effective antibiotics, but, if left untreated, the bacteria may cause neurological, kidney and cardiac problems as well as long-term trouble with walking and painful joints.

S. E. M. BY DR. ANDREW SPIELMAN/PHOTOTAKE.

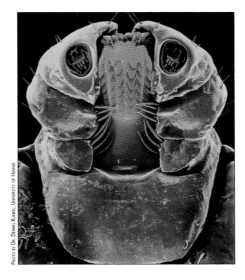

PHOTO BY DR. DENNIS KUNKEL, UNIVERSITY OF HAWAII.

The mange mite, *Psoroptes bovis*, **can infest cattle and other domestic animals.**

(sometimes called red mange or follicular mange), in which the mites live in the dog's hair follicles and sebaceous glands. This type of mange is commonly passed from the dam to her puppies and usually shows up on the puppies' muzzles, though demodicosis is not transferable from one normal dog to another. Most dogs recover from this type of mange without any treatment, though topical therapies are commonly prescribed by the vet.

The *Cheyletiellosis* mite is the hook-mouthed culprit associated with "walking dandruff," a condition that affects dogs as well as cats and rabbits. This mite lives on the surface of the animal's skin and is readily transferable through direct or indirect contact with an affected animal. The dandruff is present in the form of scaly skin, which may or may not be itchy. If not treated, this mange can affect a whole kennel of dogs and can be spread to humans as well.

The *Sarcoptes* mite causes intense itching on the dog in the form of a condition known as scabies or sarcoptic mange. The cycle of the *Sarcoptes* mite lasts about three weeks, and the mites live in the top layer of the dog's skin (epidermis), preferably in

Human lice look like dog lice; the two are closely related.

areas with little hair. Scabies is highly contagious and can be passed to humans. Sometimes an allergic reaction to the mite worsens the severe itching associated with sarcoptic mange.

Ear mites, *Otodectes cynotis,* lead to otodectic mange, which most commonly affects the outer ear canal of the dog, though other areas can be affected as well. Dogs with ear-mite infestation commonly scratch at their ears, causing further irritation, and shake their heads. Dark brown droppings in the outer ear confirm the diagnosis. Your vet can prescribe a treatment to flush out the ears and kill any eggs in the ears. A complete month of treatment is necessary to cure the mange.

Two other mites, less common in dogs, include *Dermanyssus gallinae* (the poultry or red mite) and *Eutrombicula alfreddugesi* (the North American mite associated with trombiculidiasis or chigger infestation). The poultry mite frequently lives on chickens, but can transfer to dogs who spend time near farm animals. Chigger infestation affects dogs in the

> **NOT A DROP TO DRINK**
> Never allow your dog to swim in polluted water or public areas where water quality can be suspect. Even perfectly clear water can harbor parasites, many of which can cause serious to fatal illnesses in canines. Areas inhabited by water-fowl and other wildlife are especially dangerous.

central US who have exposure to woodlands. The types of mange caused by both of these mites are treatable by veterinarians.

INTERNAL PARASITES

Most animals—fishes, birds and mammals, including dogs and humans—have worms and other parasites that live inside their bodies. According to Dr. Herbert R. Axelrod, the fish pathologist, there are two kinds of parasites: dumb and smart. The smart parasites live in peaceful cooperation with their hosts (symbiosis), while the dumb parasites kill their hosts. Most worm infections are relatively easy to control. If they are not controlled, they weaken the host dog to the point that other medical problems occur, but they do not kill the host as dumb parasites would.

A brown dog tick, *Rhipicephalus sanguineus*, is an uncommon but annoying tick found on dogs.

PHOTO BY CAROLINA BIOLOGICAL SUPPLY/PHOTOTAKE.

> **DO NOT MIX**
> Never mix parasite control products without first consulting your vet. Some products can become toxic when combined with others and can cause fatal consequences.

125

The roundworm *Rhabditis* can infect both dogs and humans.

The roundworm, *Ascaris lumbricoides*.

ROUNDWORMS

Average-size dogs can pass 1,360,000 roundworm eggs every day. For example, if there were only 1 million dogs in the world, the world would be saturated with thousands of tons of dog feces. These feces would contain around 15,000,000,000 roundworm eggs.

Up to 31% of home yards and children's sand boxes in the US contain roundworm eggs.

Flushing dog's feces down the toilet is not a safe practice because the usual sewage treatments do not destroy roundworm eggs.

Infected puppies start shedding roundworm eggs at three weeks of age. They can be infected by their mother's milk.

ROUNDWORMS

The roundworms that infect dogs are known scientifically as *Toxocara canis*. They live in the dog's intestines and shed eggs continually. It has been estimated that a dog produces about 6 or more ounces of feces every day. Each ounce of feces averages hundreds of thousands of roundworm eggs. There are no known areas in which dogs roam that do not contain roundworm eggs. The greatest danger of roundworms is that they infect people, too! It is wise to have your dog tested regularly for round-worms.

In young puppies, roundworms cause bloated bellies, diarrhea, coughing and vomiting, and are transmitted from the dam (through blood or milk). Affected puppies will not appear as animated as normal puppies. The worms appear spaghetti-like, measuring as long as 6 inches. Adult dogs can acquire roundworms through coprophagia (eating contaminated feces) or by killing rodents that carry roundworms.

Roundworm infection can kill puppies and cause severe problems in adults, as the hatched larvae travel to the lungs and trachea through the bloodstream. Cleanliness is the best preventative for roundworms. Always pick up after your dog and dispose of feces in appropriate receptacles.

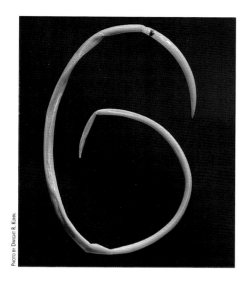

HOOKWORMS

In the United States, dog owners have to be concerned about four different species of hookworm, the most common and most serious of which is *Ancylostoma caninum,* which prefers warm climates. The others are *Ancylostoma braziliense, Ancylostoma tubaeforme* and *Uncinaria stenocephala,* the latter of which is a concern to dogs living in the northern US and Canada, as this species prefers cold climates. Hookworms are dangerous to humans as well as to dogs and cats, and can be the cause of severe anemia due to iron deficiency. The worm uses its teeth to attach itself to the dog's intestines and changes the site of its attachment about six times per day. Each time the worm repositions itself, the dog loses blood and can become anemic. *Ancylostoma caninum* is the most likely of the four species to cause anemia in the dog.

Symptoms of hookworm infection include dark stools, weight loss, general weakness, pale coloration and anemia, as well as possible skin problems. Fortunately, hookworms are easily purged from the affected dog with a number of medications that have proven effective. Discuss these with your veterinarian. Most heartworm preventatives include a hookworm insecticide as well.

Owners also must be aware that hookworms can infect humans, who can acquire the larvae through exposure to contaminated feces. Since the worms cannot complete their life cycle on a human, the worms simply infest the skin and cause irritation. This condition is known as cutaneous larva migrans syndrome. As a preventative, use disposable gloves or a "poop-scoop" to pick up your dog's droppings and prevent your dog (or neighborhood cats) from defecating in children's play areas.

The hookworm *Ancylostoma caninum.*

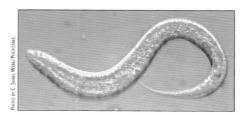

The infective stage of the hookworm larva.

127

TAPEWORMS

Humans, rats, squirrels, foxes, coyotes, wolves and domestic dogs are all susceptible to tapeworm infection. Except in humans, tapeworms are usually not a fatal infection. Infected individuals can harbor 1000 parasitic worms.

Tapeworms, like some other types of worm, are hermaphroditic, meaning male and female in the same worm.

If dogs eat infected rats or mice, or anything else infected with tapeworm, they get the tapeworm disease. One month after attaching to a dog's intestine, the worm starts shedding eggs. These eggs are infective immediately. Infective eggs can live for a few months without a host animal.

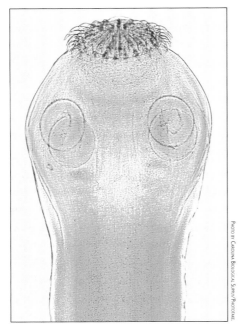

The head and rostellum (the round prominence on the scolex) of a tapeworm, which infects dogs and humans.

PHOTO BY CAROLINA BIOLOGICAL SUPPLY/PHOTOTAKE

TAPEWORMS

There are many species of tapeworm, all of which are carried by fleas! The most common tapeworm affecting dogs is known as *Dipylidium caninum*. The dog eats the flea and starts the tapeworm cycle. Humans can also be infected with tapeworms—so don't eat fleas! Fleas are so small that your dog could pass them onto your hands, your plate or your food and thus make it possible for you to ingest a flea that is carrying tapeworm eggs.

While tapeworm infection is not life-threatening in dogs (smart parasite!), it can be the cause of a very serious liver disease for humans. About 50% of the humans infected with *Echinococcus multilocularis*, a type of tapeworm that causes alveolar hydatid, perish.

WHIPWORMS

In North America, whipworms are counted among the most common parasitic worms in dogs. The whipworm's scientific name is *Trichuris vulpis*. These worms attach themselves in the lower parts of the intestine, where they feed. Affected dogs may only experience upset tummies, colic and diarrhea. These worms, however, can live for months or years in the dog, beginning their larval stage in the small intestine, spending their adult stage in the large intestine and finally passing infective eggs through the dog's feces. The only way to detect whipworms is through a fecal examination, though this is not always foolproof. Treatment for whipworms is tricky, due to the worms' unusual life-cycle pattern, and very often dogs are reinfected due to exposure to infective eggs on the ground. The whipworm eggs can survive in the environment for as long as five years, thus cleaning up droppings in your own backyard as well as in public places is absolutely essential for sanitation purposes and the health of your dog.

THREADWORMS

Though less common than roundworms, hookworms and those listed above, threadworms concern dog owners in the southwestern US and Gulf Coast area, where the climate is hot and humid. Living in the small intestine of the dog, this worm measures a mere 2 millimeters and is round in shape. Like that of the whipworm, the threadworm's life cycle is very complex and the eggs and larvae are passed through the feces. A deadly disease in humans, *Strongyloides* readily infects people, and the handling of feces is the most common means of transmission. Threadworms are most often seen in young puppies; bloody diarrhea and pneumonia are symptoms. Sick puppies must be isolated and treated immediately; vets recommend a follow-up treatment one month later.

HEARTWORM PREVENTATIVES

There are many heartworm preventatives on the market, many of which are sold at your veterinarian's office. These products can be given daily or monthly, depending on the manufacturer's instructions. All of these preventatives contain chemical insecticides directed at killing heartworms, which leads to some controversy among dog owners. In effect, heartworm preventatives are necessary evils, though you should determine how necessary based on your pet's lifestyle. There is no doubt that heartworm is a dreadful disease that threatens the lives of dogs. However, the likelihood of your dog's being bitten by an infected mosquito is slim in most places, and a mosquito-repellent (or an herbal remedy such as Wormwood or Black Walnut) is much safer for your dog and will not compromise his immune system (the way heartworm preventatives will). Should you decide to use the traditional preventative "medications," you can consider giving the pill every other or third month. Since the toxins in the pill will kill the heartworms at all stages of development, the pill would be effective in killing larvae, nymphs or adults and it takes four months for the larvae to reach the adult stage. Thus, there is no rationale to poisoning the dog's system on a monthly basis. Lastly, do not give the pill during the winter months since there are no mosquitoes around to pass on their infection, unless you live in a tropical environment.

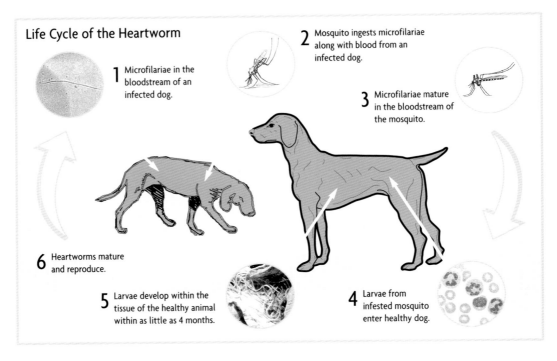

Life Cycle of the Heartworm

1 Microfilariae in the bloodstream of an infected dog.

2 Mosquito ingests microfilariae along with blood from an infected dog.

3 Microfilariae mature in the bloodstream of the mosquito.

4 Larvae from infested mosquito enter healthy dog.

5 Larvae develop within the tissue of the healthy animal within as little as 4 months.

6 Heartworms mature and reproduce.

HEARTWORMS

Heartworms are thin, extended worms up to 12 inches long, which live in a dog's heart and the major blood vessels surrounding it. Dogs may have up to 200 worms. Symptoms may be loss of energy, loss of appetite, coughing, the development of a pot belly and anemia.

Heartworms are transmitted by mosquitoes. The mosquito drinks the blood of an infected dog and takes in larvae with the blood. The larvae, called microfilariae, develop within the body of the mosquito and are passed on to the next dog bitten after the larvae mature. It takes two to three weeks for the larvae to develop to the infective stage within the body of the mosquito. Dogs are usually treated at about six weeks of age and maintained on a prophylactic dose given monthly.

Blood testing for heartworms is not necessarily indicative of how seriously your dog is infected. Although this is a dangerous disease, it is not easy for a dog to be infected. Discuss the various preventatives with your vet, as there are many different types now available. Together you can decide on a safe course of prevention for your dog.

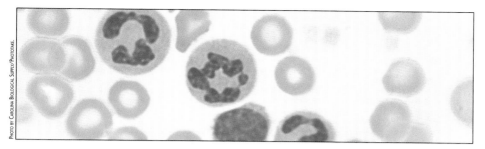

PHOTO BY CAROLINA BIOLOGICAL SUPPLY/PHOTOTAKE.

Magnified heart-worm larvae, *Diro-filaria immitis.*

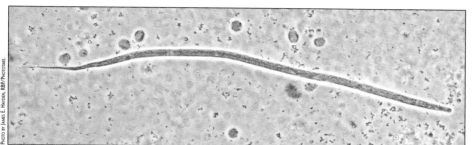

PHOTO BY JAMES E. HAYDEN, RBP/PHOTOTAKE.

Heartworm, *Diro-filaria immitis.*

PHOTO BY JAMES E. HAYDEN, RPB/PHOTOTAKE.

The heart of a dog infected with canine heart-worm, *Dirofilaria immitis.*

Neapolitan Mastiffs are prone to eye abnormalities. You should consult a veterinary ophthalmologist when you notice the early signs of any eye problems. This Neo suffers from a prominent lower central ectropion, with a medial and lateral entropion (known as "diamond-eye" syndrome, which is common in giant breeds). There is also some other source of irritation in the left eye.

Lower entropion, or rolling in of the eyelid, is causing irritation in the left eye of this young dog. Several extra eyelashes, or distichiasis, are present on the upper lid.

A PET OWNER'S GUIDE TO COMMON OPHTHALMIC DISEASES
by Prof. Dr. Robert L. Peiffer, Jr.

Few would argue that vision is the most important of the cognitive senses, and maintenance of a normal visual system is important for an optimal quality of life. Likewise, pet owners tend to be acutely aware of their pet's eyes and vision, which is important because early detection of ocular disease will optimize therapeutic outcomes. The eye is a sensitive organ with minimal reparative capabilities, and with some diseases, such as glaucoma, uveitis and retinal detachment, delay in diagnosis and treatment can be critical in terms of whether vision can be preserved.

The causes of ocular disease are quite varied; the nature of dogs make them susceptible to traumatic conditions, the most common of which include proptosis of the globe, cat scratch injuries and penetrating wounds from foreign objects, including sticks

and air rifle pellets. Infectious diseases caused by bacteria, viruses or fungi may be localized to the eye or part of a systemic infection. Many of the common conditions, including eyelid conformational problems, cataracts, glaucoma and retinal degenerations have a genetic basis.

Before acquiring your puppy it is important to ascertain that both parents have been examined and certified free of eye disease by a veterinary ophthalmologist. Since many of these genetic diseases can be detected early in life, acquire the pup with the condition that it pass a thorough ophthalmic examination by a qualified specialist.

LID CONFORMATIONAL ABNORMALITIES
Rolling in (entropion) or out (ectropion) of the lids tends to be a breed-related problem. Entropion can involve the upper and/or lower lids. Signs usually appear between 3 and 12 months of age. The irritation caused by the eyelid hairs rubbing on the surface of the

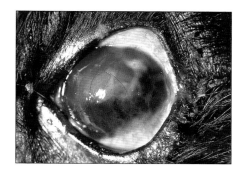

cornea may result in blinking, tearing and damage to the cornea. Ectropion is likewise breed-related and is considered "normal" in hounds, for instance; unlike entropion, which results in acute discomfort, ectropion may cause chronic irritation related to exposure and the pooling of secretions. Most of these cases can be managed medically with daily irrigation with sterile saline and topical antibiotics when required.

EYELASH ABNORMALITIES
Dogs normally have lashes only on the upper lids, in contrast to humans. Occasionally, extra eyelashes may be seen emerging at the eyelid margin (distichiasis) or through the inner surface of the eyelid (ectopic cilia).

CONJUNCTIVITIS
Inflammation of the conjunctiva, the pink tissue that lines the lids and the anterior portion of the sclera, is generally accompanied by redness, discharge and mild discomfort. The majority of cases are either associated with bacterial infections or dry eye syndrome. Fortunately, topical medications are generally effective in curing or controlling the problem.

DRY EYE SYNDROME
Dry eye syndrome (keratoconjunctivitis sicca) is a common cause of external ocular disease. Discharge is typically thick and sticky, and keratitis is a frequent component; any breed can be affected. While some cases can be associated with toxic effects of drugs, including the sulfa antibiotics, the cause in the majority of the cases cannot be determined and is assumed to be immune-mediated.

Keratoconjunctivitis sicca, seen here in the right eye of a middle-aged dog, causes a characteristic thick mucus discharge as well as secondary corneal changes.

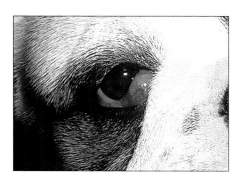

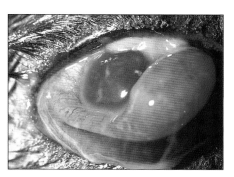

Left: Prolapse of the gland of the third eyelid in the right eye of a pup. Right: In this case, in the right eye of a young dog, the prolapsed gland can be seen emerging between the edge of the third eyelid and the corneal surface.

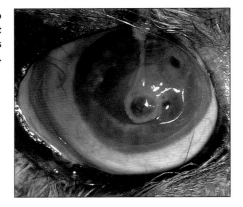

Multiple deep ulcerations affect the cornea of this middle-aged dog.

Lipid deposition can occur as a primary inherited dystrophy, or secondarily to hypercholesterolemia (in dogs frequently associated with hypothyroidism), chronic corneal inflammation or neoplasia. The deposits in this dog assume an oval pattern in the centre of the cornea.

PROLAPSE OF THE GLAND OF THE THIRD EYELID

In this condition, commonly referred to as cherry eye, the gland of the third eyelid, which produces about one-third of the aqueous phase of the tear film and is normally situated within the anterior orbit, prolapses to emerge as a pink fleshy mass protruding over the edge of the third eyelid, between the third eyelid and the cornea. The condition usually develops during the first year of life and, while mild irritation may result, the condition is unsightly as much as anything else.

CORNEAL DISEASE

The cornea is the clear front part of the eye that provides the first step in the collection of light on its journey to be eventually focused onto the retina, and most corneal diseases will be manifested by alterations in corneal transparency. The cornea is an exquisitely innervated tissue, and

defects in corneal integrity are accompanied by pain, which is demonstrated by squinting.

Corneal ulcers may occur secondary to trauma or to irritation from entropion or ectopic cilia. In middle-aged or older dogs, epithelial ulcerations may occur spontaneously due to an inherent defect; these are referred to as indolent or Boxer ulcers, in recognition of the breed in which we see the condition most frequently. Infection may occur secondarily. Ulcers can be potentially blinding conditions; severity is dependent upon the size and depth of the ulcer and other complicating features.

Non-ulcerative keratitis tends to have an immune-mediated component and is managed by topical immunosuppressants, usually corticosteroids. Corneal edema can occur in elderly dogs. It is due to a failure of the corneal endothelial "pump."

The cornea responds to chronic irritation by transforming into skin-like tissue that is

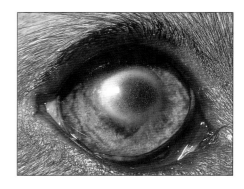

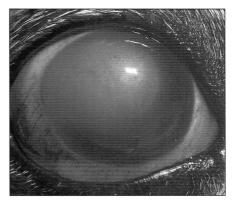

evident clinically by pigmentation, scarring and vascularization; some cases may respond to tear stimulants, lubricants and topical corticosteroids, while others benefit from surgical narrowing of the eyelid opening in order to enhance corneal protection.

UVEITIS

Inflammation of the vascular tissue of the eye–the uvea—is a common and potentially serious disease in dogs. While it may occur secondarily to trauma or other intraocular diseases, such as

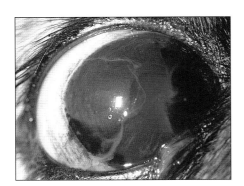

cataracts, most commonly uveitis is associated with some type of systemic infectious or neoplastic process. Uncontrolled, uveitis can lead to blinding cataracts, glaucoma and/or retinal detachments, and aggressive symptomatic therapy with dilating agents (to prevent pupillary adhesions) and anti-inflammatories are critical.

GLAUCOMA

The eye is essentially a hollow fluid-filled sphere, and the pressure within is maintained by regulation of the rate of fluid production and fluid egress at 10–20 mms. of mercury. The retinal cells are extremely sensitive to elevations of intraocular pressure and, unless controlled, permanent blindness can occur within hours to days. In acute glaucoma, the conjunctiva becomes congested, the cornea cloudy, the pupil moderate and fixed; the eye is generally painful and avisual. Increased constant signs of

Corneal edema can develop as a slowly progressive process in elderly Boston Terriers, Miniature Dachshunds and Miniature Poodles, as well as others, as a result of the inability of the corneal endothelial "pump" to maintain a state of dehydration.

Medial pigmentary keratitis in this dog is associated with irritation from prominent facial folds.

135

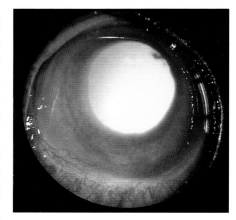

Glaucoma in the dog most commonly occurs as a sudden extreme elevation of intraocular pressure, frequently to three to four times the norm. The eye of this dog demonstrates the common signs of episcleral injection, or redness; mild diffuse corneal cloudiness, due to edema; and a mid-sized fixed pupil.

discomfort will accompany chronic cases.

Management of glaucoma is one of the most challenging situations the veterinary ophthalmologist faces; in spite of intense efforts, many of these cases will result in blindness.

CATARACTS AND LENS DISLOCATION

Cataracts are the most common blinding condition in dogs; fortunately, they are readily amenable to surgical intervention, with excellent results in terms of restoration of vision and replace-

ment of the cataractous lens with a synthetic one. Most cataracts in dogs are inherited; less commonly cataracts can be secondary to trauma, other ocular diseases, including uveitis, glaucoma, lens luxation and retinal degeneration, or secondary to an underlying systemic metabolic disease, including diabetes and Cushing's disease. Signs include a progressive loss of the bright dark appearance of the pupil, which is replaced by a blue-gray hazy appearance. In this respect, cataracts need to be distinguished from the normal aging process of nuclear sclerosis, which occurs in middle-aged or older animals, and has minimal effect on vision.

Lens dislocation occurs in dogs and frequently leads to secondary glaucoma; early removal of the dislocated lens is generally curative.

RETINAL DISEASE

Retinal degenerations are usually inherited, but may be associated with vitamin E deficiency in dogs.

Left: The typical posterior subcapsular cataract appears between one and two years of age, but rarely progresses to where the animal has visual problems. Right: Inherited cataracts generally appear between three and six years of age, and progress to the stage seen where functional vision is significantly impaired.

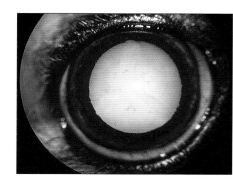

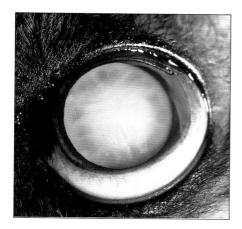

While signs are variable, most frequently one notes a decrease in vision over a period of months, which typically starts out as a night blindness. The cause of a more rapid loss of vision due to retinal degeneration occurs over days to weeks is labeled sudden acquired retinal degeneration or SARD; the outcome, however, is unfortunately usually similar to inherited and nutritional conditions, as the reti-

nal tissues possess minimal regenerative capabilities. Most pets, however, with a bit of extra care and attention, show an amazing ability to adapt to an avisual world, and can be maintained as pets with a satisfactory quality of life.

Detachment of the retina—due to accumulation of blood between the retina and the underling uvea, which is called the *choroid*—can occur secondarily to retinal tears or holes, tractional forces within the eye, or as a result of uveitis. These types of detachments may be amenable to surgical repair if diagnosed early.

OPTIC NEURITIS

Optic neuritis, or inflammation of the nerve that connects the eye with the brain stem, is a relatively uncommon condition that presents usually with rather sudden loss of vision and widely dilated non-responsive pupils.

Anterior lens luxation can occur as a primary disease in the terrier breeds, or secondarily to trauma. The fibres that hold the lens in place rupture and the lens may migrate through the pupil to be situated in front of the iris. Secondary glaucoma is a frequent and significant complication that can be avoided if the dislocated lens is removed surgically.

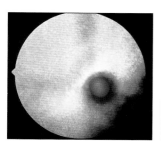
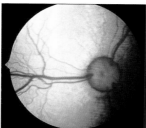
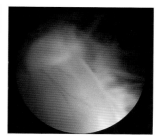

Left: The posterior pole of a normal fundus is shown; prominent are the head of the optic nerve and the retinal blood vessels. The retina is transparent, and the prominent green tapetum is seen superiorly.
Centre: An eye with inherited retinal dysplasia is depicted. The tapetal retina superior to the optic disc is disorganized, with multifocal areas of hyperplasia of the retinal pigment epithelium.
Right: Severe collie eye anomaly and a retinal detachment; this eye is unfortunately blind.

NEAPOLITAN MASTIFF

When you purchase your Neapolitan Mastiff, you will make it clear to the breeder whether you want one just as a lovable companion and pet, or if you hope to be buying a Neapolitan Mastiff with show prospects. No reputable breeder will sell you a young puppy and tell you that it is definitely of show quality, for so much can go wrong during the early months of a puppy's development. If you plan to show, what you will hopefully have acquired is a puppy with "show potential."

To the novice, exhibiting a Neapolitan Mastiff in the show ring may look easy, but it takes a lot of hard work and devotion to do top winning at a show such as the Westminster Kennel Club show or the World Dog Show, not to mention a little luck too!

The first concept that the canine novice learns when watching a dog show is that each dog first competes against members of his own breed. Once the judge has selected the best member of each breed (Best of Breed), provided that the show is judged on a Group system, that chosen dog will compete with other dogs in his group. Finally, the dogs chosen first in each group will compete for Best in Show.

The second concept that you must understand is that the dogs are

MEET THE AKC

The American Kennel Club is the main governing body of the dog sport in the United States. Founded in 1884, the AKC consists of 500 or more independent dog clubs plus 4,500 affiliated clubs, all of which follow the AKC rules and regulations. Additionally, the AKC maintains a registry for pure-bred dogs in the US and works to preserve the integrity of the sport and its continuation in the country. Over 1,000,000 dogs are registered each year, representing about 150 recognized breeds. There are over 15,000 competitive events held annually for which over 2,000,000 dogs enter to participate. Dogs compete to earn over 40 different titles, from champion to Companion Dog to Master Agility Champion.

not actually compared against one another. The judge compares each dog against his breed standard, the written description of the ideal specimen that is approved by a major kennel club like the Fédération Cynologique Internationale (FCI) or the American Kennel Club (AKC). While some early breed standards were indeed based on specific dogs that were famous or popular, many dedicated enthusiasts say that a perfect specimen, as described in the standard, has never walked into a show ring, has never been bred and, to the woe of dog breeders around the globe, does not exist. Breeders attempt to get as close to this ideal as possible with every litter, but theoretically the "perfect" dog is so elusive that it is impossible. (And if the "perfect" dog were born, breeders and judges would never agree that it was indeed "perfect.")

If you are interested in exploring the world of dog showing, your best bet is to join your local breed club or the parent club, which is the United States Neapolitan Mastiff Club. These clubs often host both regional and national specialties, shows only for Neapolitan Mastiffs, which can include conformation as well as obedience and agility trials. Even if you have no intention of competing with your Neapolitan Mastiff, a specialty is like a festival for lovers of the breed who congregate to share their favorite topic: Neos! Clubs also send out newslet-

Dignified and regal in bearing, the massive Neapolitan Mastiff makes an impressive show dog. Although this is not a "showy" breed, it certainly has a unique presence in the ring.

ters, and some organize training days and seminars in order that people may learn more about their chosen breed. To locate the breed club closest to you, contact the American Kennel Club, which furnishes the rules and regulations for many events for the breed.

If your Neapolitan Mastiff is six months of age or older and registered with the club, you can enter him in a dog show where the breed is offered classes. Provided that your Neapolitan Mastiff does not have a disqualifying fault, he can compete. Only unaltered dogs can be entered in a dog show, so if you have spayed or neutered your Neapolitan Mastiff, your dog cannot compete in conformation shows.

The reason for this is simple. Dog shows are the main forum to prove which representatives in a breed are worthy of being bred. Only dogs that have achieved championships—the dog world's

139

"seal of approval" for quality in pure-bred dogs—should be bred. Altered dogs, however, can participate in other events such as obedience trials.

Before you actually step into the ring, you would be well advised to sit back and observe the judge's ring procedure. If it is your first time in the ring, do not be over-anxious and run to the front of the line. It is much better to stand back and study how the exhibitor in front of you is performing. The judge asks each handler to "stack" the dog, hopefully showing the dog off to his best advantage. The judge will observe the dog from a distance and from different angles, and approach the dog to check his teeth, overall structure, alertness and muscle tone, as well as consider how well the dog "conforms" to the standard. Most importantly, the judge will have the exhibitor move the dog around the ring in some pattern that he should specify. Finally, the judge will give the dog one last look before moving on to the next exhibitor.

If you are not in the top four in your class at your first show, do not be discouraged. Be patient and consistent, and you may eventually find yourself in a winning line-up. Remember that the winners were once in your shoes and have devoted many hours and much money to earn the placement. If you find that your dog is losing every time and never getting a nod, it may

be time to consider a different dog sport or to just enjoy your Neapolitan Mastiff as a pet. Parent clubs offer other events, such as agility, tracking, obedience, instinct tests and more, which may be of interest to the owner of a well-trained Neapolitan Mastiff.

HOW SHOWS ARE ORGANIZED

Three kinds of conformation shows are offered by the AKC. There is the all-breed show, in which all AKC-recognized breeds can compete; the specialty show, which is for one breed only and usually sponsored by the breed's parent club and the

INFORMATION ON CLUBS

You can get information about dog shows from the national kennel clubs:
American Kennel Club
5580 Centerview Dr.,
Raleigh, NC 27606-3390
www.akc.org

United Kennel Club
100 E. Kilgore Road, Kalamazoo, MI 49002
www.ukcdogs.com

Canadian Kennel Club
89 Skyway Ave., Suite 100, Etobicoke,
Ontario M9W 6R4 Canada
www.ckc.ca

The Kennel Club
1-5 Clarges St., Piccadilly, London
W1Y 8AB UK
www.the-kennel-club.org.uk

Fédération Cynologique Internationale
14, rue Leopold II, B-6530 Thuin, Belgium
www.fci.be

group show, for all breeds in one of the AKC's seven groups. The Neapolitan Mastiff competes in the Working Group.

For a dog to become an AKC champion of record, the dog must earn 15 points at shows. The points must be awarded by at least three different judges and must include two "majors" under different judges. A "major" is a three-, four- or five-point win, and the number of points per win is determined by the number of dogs competing in the show on that day. (Dogs that are absent or are excused are not counted.) The number of points that are awarded varies from breed to breed. More dogs are needed to attain a major in more popular breeds, and fewer dogs are needed in less popular breeds. Yearly, the AKC evaluates the number of dogs in competition in each division (there are 14 divisions in all, based on geography) and may or may not change the numbers of dogs required for each number of points. For example, a major in Division 2 (Delaware, New Jersey and Pennsylvania) recently required 17 dogs or 16 bitches for a three-point major, 29 dogs or 27 bitches for a four-point major and 51 dogs or 46 bitches for a five-point major. Compared to the top 20 AKC breeds, the Neo does not attract large numbers at most all-breed shows.

Only one dog and one bitch of each breed can win points at a

given show. There are no "co-ed" classes except for champions of record. Dogs and bitches do not compete against each other until they are champions. Dogs that are not champions (referred to as "class dogs") compete in one of five classes. The class in which a dog is entered depends on age and previous show wins. First there is the Puppy Class (sometimes divided further into classes for 6- to 9-month-olds and 9- to 12-month-olds); next is the Novice Class (for dogs that have no points toward their championship and whose only first-place wins have come in the Puppy Class or the Novice Class, the latter class limited to three first places); then there is the American-bred Class (for dogs bred in the US); the Bred-by-Exhibitor Class (for dogs handled by their breeders or by immediate family members of their breeders) and the

Neapolitan Mastiffs being judged in a special Brace Class at an international championship show. Notice that two handlers were needed (usually only one handler escorts the brace).

141

The proper gait for the Neo is slow, free and bear-like. Although he does not move quickly, the Neo covers a lot of ground with his long strides.

Open Class (for any non-champions). Any dog may enter the Open class, regardless of age or win history, but to be competitive the dog should be older and have ring experience.

The judge at the show begins judging the male dogs in the Puppy Class(es) and proceeds through the other classes. The judge awards first through fourth place in each class. The first-place winners of each class then compete with one another in the Winners Class to determine Winners Dog. The judge then starts over with the bitches, beginning with the Puppy Class(es) and proceeding up to the Winners Class to award Winners Bitch, just as he did with the dogs. A Reserve Winners Dog and Reserve Winners Bitch are also selected; they could be awarded the points in the case of a disqualification.

The Winners Dog and Winners Bitch are the two that are awarded

MEETING THE IDEAL

The American Kennel Club defines a standard as: "A description of the ideal dog of each recognized breed, to serve as an ideal against which dogs are judged at shows." This "blueprint" is drawn up by the breed's recognized parent club, approved by a majority of its membership, and then submitted to the AKC for approval. This is a complete departure from the way standards are handled in the UK, where all standards and changes are controlled by The Kennel Club.

The AKC states that "An understanding of any breed must begin with its standard. This applies to all dogs, not just those intended for showing." The picture that the standard draws of the dog's type, gait, temperament and structure is the guiding image used by breeders as they plan their programs.

the points for their breed. They then go on to compete with any champions of record (often called "specials") of their breed that are entered in the show. The champions may be dogs or bitches; in this class, all are shown together. The judge reviews the Winners Dog and Winners Bitch along with all of the champions to select the Best of Breed winner. The Best of Winners is selected between the Winners Dog and Winners Bitch; if one of these two is selected Best of Breed as well, he or she is automatically determined Best of Winners. Lastly, the judge selects Best of Opposite Sex to the Best of Breed winner. The Best of Breed winner then goes on to the Group competition.

SHOW QUALITY SHOWS

While you may purchase a puppy in the hope of having a successful career in the show ring, it is impossible to tell, at eight to ten weeks of age, whether your dog will be a contender. Some promising pups end up with minor to serious faults that prevent them from taking home an award, but this certainly does not mean they can't be the best of companions for you and your family. To find out if your potential show dog is show-quality, enter him in a match to see how a judge evaluates him. You may also take him back to your breeder as he matures to see what the breeder might advise.

If your Neapolitan Mastiff is of show quality, you may want to give conformation showing a try.

At a Group or all-breed show, the Best of Breed winners from each breed are divided into their respective groups to compete against one another for Group One through Group Four. Group One (first place) is awarded to the dog that best lives up to the ideal for his breed as described in the standard. A Group judge, therefore, must have a thorough working knowledge of many breed standards. After placements have been made in each Group, the seven Group One winners (from the Working Group, Toy Group, Hound Group, etc.) compete against each other for the top honor, Best in Show.

There are different ways to find out about dog shows in your area. The American Kennel Club's monthly magazine, the *American Kennel Gazette* is accompanied by, the *Events Calendar*; this magazine is available through subscription. You can also look on the AKC's and the USNMC's websites for information and check the event listings in your local newspaper.

143

NEAPOLITAN MASTIFF

As a Neapolitan Mastiff owner, you selected your dog so that you and your loved ones could have a companion, a protector, a friend and a four-legged family member. You invest time, money and effort to care for and train the family's new charge. Of course, this chosen canine behaves perfectly! Well, perfectly like a dog. When discussing the Neapolitan Mastiff, owners have much to consider.

THINK LIKE A DOG

Dogs do not think like humans, nor do humans think like dogs, though we try. Unfortunately, a dog is incapable of figuring out how humans think, so the responsibility falls on the owner to adopt a viable canine mindset. Dogs cannot rationalize, and they only exist in the present moment. Many dog owners make the mistake in training of thinking that they can reprimand their dog for something he did a while ago. Basically, you cannot even reprimand a dog for something he did 20 seconds ago! Either catch him in the act or forget it! It is a waste of your and your dog's time—in his mind, you are reprimanding him for whatever he is doing at that moment.

The following behavioral problems represent some which owners most commonly encounter. Every dog is unique and every situation is unique. No author could purport for you to solve your Neapolitan Mastiff's problem simply by reading a chapter in a breed book. Here we outline some basic "dogspeak" so that owners' chances of solving behavioral problems are increased. Discuss bad habits with your veterinarian and he can recommend a behavioral specialist to consult in appropriate cases. Since behavioral abnormalities are the leading reason owners abandon their pets, we hope that you will make a valiant effort to solve your Neapolitan Mastiff's problem. Patience and understanding are

SET AN EXAMPLE

Never scream, shout, jump or run about if you want your dog to stay calm. You set the example for your dog's behavior in most circumstances. Learn from your dog's reaction to your behavior and act accordingly.

virtues that dwell in every pet-loving household.

AGGRESSION

Aggression is a problem that concerns owners of all dogs, and Neapolitan Mastiffs are no exception. Aggression can be a very big problem in dogs, even more so in a very large breed like the Neapolitan. Aggression, when not controlled, always becomes dangerous. An aggressive dog, no matter the size, may lunge at, bite or even attack a person or another dog. Aggressive behavior is not to be tolerated. It is more than just inappropriate behavior; it is not safe, especially with a large breed such as the Neapolitan Mastiff. It is painful for a family to watch its dog become unpredictable in his behavior to the point where they are afraid of him. While not all aggressive behavior is dangerous, growling, baring teeth, etc., can be frightening. It is important to ascertain why the dog is acting in this manner. Aggression is a display of dominance, and the dog should not have the dominant role in his pack, which is, in this case, your family.

It is important not to challenge an aggressive dog as this could provoke an attack. Observe your Neapolitan Mastiff's body language. Does he make direct eye contact and stare? Does he try to make himself as large as possible: ears pricked, chest out, tail erect?

Height and size signify authority in a dog pack—being taller or "above" another dog literally means that he is "above" in the social status. These body signals tell you that your Neapolitan Mastiff thinks he is in charge, a problem that needs to be addressed. An aggressive dog is unpredictable: you never know when he is going to strike and what he is going to do. You cannot understand why a dog that

"My back doesn't itch...I want my belly scratched." Being able to read doggie language comes from experience.

IT'S PLAY TIME

Physical games like pulling contests, wrestling, jumping and teasing should not be encouraged. Inciting a dog's crazy behavior tends to confuse him. The owner has to be able to control his dog at all times. Even in play, your dog has to know that you are the leader and that you decide when to play and when to behave mannerly.

is playful and loving one minute is growling and snapping the next.

The best solution is to consult a behavioral specialist, one who has experience with the Neapolitan Mastiff if possible. Together, perhaps you can pinpoint the cause of your dog's aggression and do something about it. An aggressive dog cannot be trusted, and a dog that cannot be trusted is not safe to have as a family pet. If, very unusually, you find that your pet has become untrustworthy and you feel it necessary to seek a new home with a more suitable family and environment, explain fully to the new owners all your reasons for rehoming the dog to be fair to all concerned. In the very worst case, you will have to consider euthanasia.

AGGRESSION TOWARD OTHER DOGS
A dog's aggressive behavior toward another dog sometimes stems from insufficient exposure to other dogs

at an early age. If other dogs make your Neapolitan Mastiff nervous and agitated, he will lash out as a defensive mechanism, though this behavior is thankfully uncommon in the breed. A dog who has not received sufficient exposure to other canines tends to believe that he is the only dog on the planet. The animal becomes so dominant that he does not even show signs that he is fearful or threatened. Without growling or any other physical signal as a warning, he will lunge at and bite the other dog. A way to correct this is to let your Neapolitan Mastiff approach another dog when walking on lead. Watch very closely and at the very first sign of aggression, correct your Neapolitan Mastiff and pull him away. Scold him for any sign of discomfort, and then praise him when he ignores or tolerates the other dog. Keep this up until he stops the aggressive behavior, learns to ignore the other dog or accepts other dogs. Praise him lavishly for his correct behavior.

DOMINANT AGGRESSION
A social hierarchy is firmly established in a wild dog pack. The dog wants to dominate those under him and please those above him. Dogs know that there must be a leader. If you are not the obvious choice for emperor, the dog will assume the throne! These conflicting innate desires are what a dog owner is up against when he sets

PROFESSIONAL TRAINING

If your dog barks menacingly or growls at strangers, or if he growls at anyone who comes near his food while he is eating, playing with a toy or taking a rest in his favorite spot, he needs proper professional training because sooner or later this behavior can result in someone being bitten.

AGGRESSIVE BEHAVIOR

Dog aggression is a serious problem. never give an aggressive dog to someone else. The dog will usually be more aggressive in a new situation where his leadership is unchallenged and unquestioned (in his mind).

about training a dog. In training a dog to obey commands, the owner is reinforcing that he is the top dog in the "pack" and that the dog should, and should want to, serve his superior. Thus, the owner is suppressing the dog's urge to dominate by modifying his behavior and making him obedient.

An important part of training is taking every opportunity to reinforce that you are the leader. The simple action of making your Neapolitan Mastiff sit to wait for his food says that you control when he eats and that he is dependent on you for food. Although it may be difficult, do not give in to your dog's wishes every time he whines at you or looks at you with his pleading eyes. It is a constant effort to show the dog that his place in the pack is at the bottom. This is not meant to sound cruel or inhumane. You love your Neapolitan Mastiff and you should treat him with care and affection. You did not get a dog just so you could boss around another creature. Dog training is not about being cruel or feeling important, it is about mold-

ing the dog's behavior into what is acceptable and teaching him to live by your rules. In theory, it is quite simple: catch him in appropriate behavior and reward him for it. Add a dog into the equation and it becomes a bit more trying, but as a rule of thumb, positive reinforcement is what works best.

With a dominant dog, punishment and negative reinforcement can have the opposite effect of what you are after. It can make a dog fearful and/or act out aggressively if he feels he is being challenged. Remember, a dominant dog perceives himself at the top of the social heap and will fight to defend his perceived status. The best way to prevent that is never to give him reason to think that he is

A raised knee is an often-used technique to stop a dog from jumping up. Reinforce the lesson positively by praising the dog when all four paws are on the ground.

147

Neapolitan Mastiff

This three-year-old male, bred by the author, is the picture of confidence and power. Any dog as powerful as the Neo must be controlled at all times.

FEAR IN A GROWN DOG

Fear in a grown dog is often the result of improper or incomplete socialization as a pup, or it can be the result of a traumatic experience he suffered when young. Keep in mind that the term "traumatic" is relative—something that you would not think twice about can leave a lasting negative impression on a puppy. If the dog experiences a similar experience later in life, he may try to fight back to protect himself. Again, this behavior is very unpredictable, especially if you do not know what is triggering his fear.

in control in the first place. If you are having trouble training your Neapolitan Mastiff and it seems as if he is constantly challenging your authority, seek the help of an obedience trainer or behavioral specialist. A professional will work with both you and your dog to teach you effective techniques to use at home. Beware of trainers who rely on excessively harsh methods; scolding is necessary now and then, but the focus in your training should always be on positive reinforcement.

If you can isolate what brings out the fear reaction, you can help the dog overcome it. Super-

DOMINANT AGGRESSION

Never allow your puppy to growl at you or bare his tiny teeth. Such behavior is dominant and aggressive. If not corrected, the dog will repeat the behavior, which will become more threatening as he grows larger and will eventually lead to biting.

A male dog uses urination to mark his territory. He recognizes his own scent and can smell if another dog has been there.

vise your Neapolitan Mastiff's interactions with people and other dogs, and praise the dog when it goes well. If he starts to act aggressively in a situation, correct him and remove him from the situation. Do not let people approach the dog and start petting him without your express permission. That way, you can have the dog sit to accept petting, and praise him when he behaves properly. You are focusing on praise and on modifying his behavior by rewarding him when he acts appropriately. By being gentle and by supervising his interactions, you are showing him that there is no need to be afraid or defensive.

SEXUAL BEHAVIOR

Dogs exhibit certain sexual behaviors that may have influenced your choice of male or female when you first purchased your Neapolitan Mastiff. To a certain extent, spaying/neutering will eliminate these behaviors, but if you are purchas-

ing a dog that you wish to breed, you should be aware of what you will have to deal with throughout the dog's life.

Female dogs usually have two estruses per year with each season lasting about three weeks. These are the only times in which a female dog will mate, and she usually will not allow this until the second week of the cycle, but this does vary from bitch to bitch. If not bred during the heat cycle, it is not uncommon for a bitch to experience a false pregnancy, in which her mammary glands swell and she exhibits maternal tendencies toward toys or other objects.

Owners must further recognize that mounting is not merely

149

is responsible for ensuring a dog-proof environment. The best answer is prevention: that is, put your shoes, handbags and other tasty objects in their proper places (out of the reach of the growing canine mouth). Direct puppies to their toys whenever you see them tasting the furniture legs or the leg of your pants. Make a loud noise to attract the pup's attention and immediately escort him to his chew toy and engage him with the toy for at least four minutes, praising and encouraging him all the while.

With a dog that can actually chew you out of house and home, it is wise to train the dog to use strong chew toys to save your possessions from becoming tasty options.

a sexual expression but also one of dominance. Be consistent and persistent and you will find that you can "move mounters."

CHEWING

The national canine pastime is chewing! Every dog loves to sink his "canines" into a tasty bone, but sometimes that bone is in his owner's hand! Dogs need to chew, to massage their gums, to make their new teeth feel better and to exercise their jaws. This is a natural behavior deeply imbedded in all things canine. Our role as owners is not to stop the dog's chewing, but to redirect it to positive, chew-worthy objects. Be an informed owner and purchase proper chew toys like strong nylon bones that will not splinter. Be sure that the devices are safe and durable, since your dog's safety is at risk. Again, the owner

THE MIGHTY MALE

Males, whether castrated or not, will mount almost anything: a pillow, your leg or, much to your dismay, even your neighbor's leg. As with other types of inappropriate behavior, the dog must be corrected while in the act, which for once is not difficult. Often he will not let go! While a puppy is experimenting with his very first urges, his owners feel he needs to "sow his oats" and allow the pup to mount. As the pup grows into a full-size dog, with full-size urges, it becomes a nuisance and an embarrassment. Males always appear as if they are trying to "save the race," more determined and stronger than imaginable. While altering the dog at an appropriate age will limit the dog's desire, it usually does not remove it entirely.

Some trainers recommend deterrents, such as hot pepper or another bitter spice or a product designed for this purpose, to discourage the dog from chewing unwanted objects. Test these products on your Neo before investing in a large quantity.

JUMPING UP

Jumping up is a dog's friendly way of saying hello! Some owners do not mind when their pups jump up. The problem arises when guests come to the house and the adult dog greets them in the same manner. However friendly the greeting may be, your visitors will not appreciate your 200-pound dog's enthusiasm. Therefore, it is best to discourage this behavior entirely for the safety of all involved.

Pick a command such as "Off" (avoid using "Down" since you will use that for the dog to lie down) and tell him "Off" when he jumps up. Place him on the ground on all fours and have him sit, praising him the whole time. Always lavish him with praise and petting when he is in the sit position. That way you are still giving him a warm affectionate greeting, because you are as pleased to see him as he is to see you!

DIGGING

Digging, which is seen as a destructive behavior to humans, is actually quite a natural behavior

SOUND BITES

When a dog bites, there is always a good reason for his doing so. Many dogs are trained to protect a person, an area or an object. When that person, area or object is violated, the dog will attack. A dog attacks with his mouth. He has no other means of attack.

Fighting dogs (and there are many breeds which fight) are taught to fight, but they also have a natural instinct to fight. This instinct is normally reserved for other dogs, though unfortunate accidents can occur; for example, when a baby crawls toward a fighting dog and the dog mistakes the crawling child as a potential attacker.

If a dog is a biter for seemingly no reason, if he bites the hand that feeds him or if he snaps at members of your family, see your veterinarian or behaviorist immediately to learn how to modify the dog's behavior.

in dogs. Whether or not your dog is one of the "earth dogs" (also known as terriers), his desire to dig can be irrepressible and most frustrating to his owners. When digging occurs in your garden, it is actually a normal behavior redirected into something the dog can do in his everyday life. In the wild, a dog would be actively seeking food, making his own shelter, etc. He would be using his paws in a purposeful manner for his survival. Since you provide him with food and shelter, he has no need to use his paws for these purposes, and so the energy that he would be using may manifest itself in the form of little holes all over your yard and flower beds.

Perhaps your dog is digging as a reaction to boredom—it is somewhat similar to someone eating a whole bag of chips in front of the TV—because they are there and there is not anything better to do! Basically, the answer is to provide the dog with adequate play and exercise so that his mind and paws are occupied, and so that he feels as if he is doing something useful.

Of course, digging is easiest to control if it is stopped as soon as possible, but it is often hard to catch a dog in the act. If your dog is a compulsive digger and is not easily distracted by other activi-

ties, you can designate an area on your property where it is okay for him to dig. If you catch him digging in an off-limits area of the yard, immediately bring him to the approved area and praise him for digging there. Keep a close eye on him so that you can catch him in the act—that is the only way to make him understand what is permitted and what is not. If you take him to a hole he dug an hour ago and tell him "No," he will understand that you are not fond of holes, or dirt, or flowers. If you catch him while he is stifle-deep in your tulips, that is when he will get your message.

BARKING

Dogs cannot talk—oh, what they would say if they could! Instead, barking is a dog's way of "talking." It can be somewhat frustrating because it is not always easy to tell what a dog means by his bark—is he excited, happy, frightened or angry? Whatever it is that the dog is trying to say, he should not be punished for barking. It is only when the barking becomes excessive, and when the excessive barking becomes a bad habit, that the behavior needs to be modified. Fortunately, Neapolitan Mastiffs are not as vocal as most other dogs, and they tend to use their barks more purposefully than most dogs. If an intruder came into your home in the middle of the night and your

HE'S PROTECTING YOU

Barking is your dog's way of protecting you. If he barks at a stranger walking past your house, a moving car or a fleeing cat, he is merely exercising his responsibility to protect his pack (YOU) and territory from a perceived intruder. Since the "intruder" usually keeps going, the dog thinks his barking chased it away and he feels fulfilled. This behavior leads your overly vocal friend to believe that he is the "dog in charge."

Neapolitan Mastiff barked a warning, wouldn't you be pleased? You would probably deem your dog a hero, a wonderful guardian and protector of the home. Most dogs are not as discriminate as the Neapolitan Mastiff. For instance, if a friend drops by unexpectedly and rings the doorbell and is greeted with a sudden sharp bark, you would probably be annoyed at the dog. But in reality, isn't this just the same behavior? The dog does not know any better…unless he sees who is at the door and it is someone he knows, he will bark as a means of vocalizing that his (and your) territory is being threatened.

While your friend is not posing a threat, it is all the same to the dog. Barking is his means of letting you know that there is an intrusion, whether friend or foe, on your property. This type of barking is instinctive and should not be discouraged.

Excessive habitual barking, however, is a problem that should be corrected early on. As your Neapolitan Mastiff grows up, you will be able to tell when his barking is purposeful and when it is for no reason. You will become able to distinguish your dog's different barks and their meanings. For example, the bark when someone comes to the door will

A dam may act very protective of her pups. This is instinct and usually not the sign of an aggressive dog.

be different from the bark when he is excited to see you. It is similar to a person's tone of voice, except that the dog has to rely totally on tone of voice because he does not have the benefit of using words. An incessant barker will be evident at an early age.

There are some things that encourage a dog to bark. For example, if your dog barks non-stop for a few minutes and you give him a treat to quiet him, he believes that you are rewarding him for barking. He will associate barking with getting a treat, and will keep doing it until he is rewarded.

FOOD STEALING

Is your dog devising ways of stealing food from your coffee table? If so, you must answer the following questions: Is your Neapolitan Mastiff hungry, or is he "constantly famished" like many dogs seem to be? Face it, some dogs are more food-motivated than others. Some dogs are totally obsessed by the smell of food and can only think of their next meal. Food stealing is terrific fun and always yields a great reward—food, glorious food.

The owner's goal, therefore, is to be sensible about where food is placed in the home, and to reprimand the dog whenever he is caught in the act of stealing. But remember, only reprimand the dog if you actually see him stealing, not later when the crime is discovered for that will be of no use at all and will only serve to confuse.

BEGGING

Just like food stealing, begging is a favorite pastime of hungry puppies! It yields that same great reward—*food*! Dogs quickly learn that their owners keep the "good food" for themselves, and that we humans do not dine on dry food alone. Begging is a conditioned response related to a specific stimulus, time and place. The sounds of the kitchen, cans and bottles opening, crinkling bags, the smell of food in preparation, etc., will excite the dog and soon the paws are in the air!

Here is the solution to stopping this behavior: Never give in to a beggar! You are rewarding the dog for sitting pretty, jumping up, whining and rubbing his nose into you by giving him that glorious reward—food. By ignoring the dog, you will (eventually) force the behavior into extinction. Note that the behavior likely gets worse before it disappears, so be sure there are not any "softies" in the family who will give in to little "Oliver" every time he whimpers, "More, please."

SEPARATION ANXIETY

Your Neapolitan Mastiff may howl, whine or otherwise vocalize his displeasure at your leaving the house and his being left alone. This is a normal reaction, no different from the child who cries as his mother leaves him on the first day at school. In fact, constant attention can lead to separation anxiety in the first place. If you are endlessly fussing over your dog, he will come to expect this from you all of the time and it will be more traumatic for him when you are not there. Obviously, you enjoy spending time with your dog, and he thrives on your love and attention. However, it should not become a dependent relationship where he is heartbroken without you.

One thing you can do to minimize separation anxiety is to make your entrances and exits as low-key as possible. Do not give your dog a long drawn-out good-bye, and do not lavish him with hugs and kisses when you return. This is giving in to the attention that he craves, and it will only make him miss it more when you are away. Another thing you can try is to give your dog a treat when you leave; this will not only keep him occupied and keep his mind off the fact that you have just left, but it will also help him associate your leaving with a pleasant experience.

You may have to accustom your dog to being left alone in intervals. Of course, when your dog starts whimpering as you approach the door, your first instinct will be to run to him and comfort him, but do not do it! Really—eventually he will adjust and be just fine if you take it in small steps. His anxiety stems from being placed in an unfamiliar situation; by familiarizing him with being alone he will learn that he is okay. That is not to say you should purposely leave your dog home alone, but the dog needs to know that while he can depend on you for his care, you do not have to be by his side 24 hours a day.

When the dog is alone in the house, he should be confined to his designated dog-proof area of the house. This should be the area in which he sleeps and already feels comfortable so he will feel more at ease when he is alone.

"LONELY WOLF"

The number of dogs that suffer from separation anxiety is on the rise as more and more pet owners find themselves at work all day. New attention is being paid to this problem, which is especially hard to diagnose since it is only evident when the dog is alone. Research is currently being done to help educate dog owners about separation anxiety and how they can help minimize this problem in their dogs.

INDEX

*Page numbers in **boldface** indicate illustrations.*

Acral lick 114
Adult diet 68
Age 85
Aggression 145
—dominant 147
—toward other dogs 146
Agility 142
Alexander the Great 9
Allergies
—airborne 114
—food 115
Alpha dog 20
American Kennel Club 28, 138, 140-143
—address 140
—*Gazette* 143
Ancylostoma caninum 127
Anesthesia 27
Aronne 12
Ascaris lumbricoides **126**
Attila della Grotta Azzurra 12
Axelrod, Dr. Herbert R. 127
Backpacking 103
Barking 152
Bathing 71
Bedding 27, 44
Begging 154
Behavioral problems 144
Bloat 107
Boarding 77
Body language 145
Bones 46, 150
Boredom 152
Bowls 48, **50**
Breeder 34
British Isles 9
Brown dog tick **125**
Brushing 70
Caesar, Julius 9
Califf della Dea Partenopea 12
Canadian Kennel Club
—address 140
Cancer 117
Canine cough 110-111
Cars 75
Cat 93
Cataracts **136**
Champion 141
Cherry eye 25, 134

Chew toys 150
Chewing 22, 87, 150
Cheyletiella 125
Chicago Art Museum 9
Children 20
Choke collars 48
Coat 17
Collar 47, **49**, 93
Colostrum 65
Colors 17
Columella 10
Come 99
Commands 95
Companion dog 23
Conjunctivitis 133
Coronavirus 111
Corneal disease 134
Corneal edema **135**
Crate 41, **43**, 61, 76, 86, 90
—training 90
Crying 61
Ctenocephalides canis **118, 120**
De Re Rustica 10
Demodicosis 24
Demodectic mange 24
Demodex 24, 123
Dermacentor variabilis **122, 123**
Destructive behavior 154
Development schedule 85
Deworming program 127
Diamond-eye syndrome 132
Diet 62
—adult 68
—puppy 64
—senior 68
Digging 152
Dirofilaria immitis **130, 131**
Discipline 92
Distemper 111
Dog flea **118, 121**
Dog tick **125**
Dominance 20
Down 96
Drooling 22
Dry eye 133
Ear 18
—cleaning 72
—mite 125
Echinococcus multilocularis **130**

Ectropion 27, **132**
Elbow dysplasia 25
Enea di Ponzano 12
Entropion 27, **132**
Estrus 149
Exercise 24, 69
External parasites 118-125
Eyelash abnormalities 133
Eyes 17
—problems 132-137
Falco della Grotta Azzurra 11
Fear period 56
Fédération Cynologique
    Internationale 28
—address 140
—standard 16
Feeding 62
Fence 52
Field trials 142
First aid 116
Flea 118-122
—life cycle 119, **121**
Food 63
—allergy 115
—intolerance 115, 117
—problems 115
—stealing 154
—treats 102
Football injury 25
Frazier della Grotta Azzurra 13
Gastric torsion 107
Gavilan dell'Altafiumara 13
Germany 11-12
Gilda di Ponzano 12
Glaucoma 135, **136**
Grooming 17
Guard dog 10, 23
Handling 141
Hair **73**
Hatrim della Grotta Azzurra 13
Health considerations 24
Heartworm 130
—life cycle 130
—preventative 129
Heat stroke 27
Heel 100
Height 16
Hepatitis 111
Hereditary diseases 24

Hip dysplasia 25, 26
Home preparation 40
Hookworm 127
—larva **127**
Housebreaking 82
—schedule 89
Hunting dog 10
Identification 79
Internal parasites 125-131
International Beauty Champion 142
International Champion 142
International Trial Champion 142
Italian Kennel Club 11
Ixode 125
Judge 140
Jumping up 151
Kennel 35
Kennel Club, The 28
—address 140
Keratoconjunctivitis sicca **133**
Kuhn, Dwight R. 122
Lead 46, 93
Lens dislocation 136, 137
Leone 11
Leptospirosis 111
Lice **124**
Life span 17
Loyalty 19
Lupus 113
Lyme disease 123
Madigam della Grotta Azzurra 11
Mange 125
Mange mite 24, 126
Mason della Grotta Azzurra 12
Mastinari 15
Mastino Napoletano 11
Matches 139, 141
Maturation 17
Medea della Grotta Azzurra 12
Metropolitan Museum 9
Milk 65
Mite 123, 125
—infestation 72
Mollosers 9
Molosso Romano 11
Mosé 13
Mounting 150
Mt. Vesuvius 10
Nail clipping 72
Neapolitan Mastiff Club of America 12
Negative reinforcement 148
Nerone 12

Neutering 110
Nipping 58
Obedience class 80, 102
Obedience work 23
Obesity 69
Off 151
Open shows 139-140
Optic neuritis 137
Oro 12
Ownership 37
Pacchiana 12
Pain tolerance 24
Panosteitis 27
Parasite
—bite 113
—external 118-125
—internal 125-131
Parvovirus 111
Personality 19
Phoenicians 9
Physical characteristics 16
Pollen allergy 114
Prolapsed gland **133,** 134
Protein 62
Psoroptes bovis **124**
Pugnaces Brittaniae 9
Punishment 93, 148, 150
Puppy
—family introduction 53
—first night home 54
—food 64
—health 107
—problems 55, 58
—training 81
Puppy-proofing 51
Rabies 111
Registration 38
Renaissance 10
Retinal disease 136, **137**
Rhabditis **127**
Rhipicephalus sanguineus **125**
Roman Empire 10
Romana della Grotta Azzurra 12
Roundworm 126
Ruptured anterior cruciate ligament 25
Sansone I di Ponzano 11
SARD 137
Sarno 12
Seasonal cycles 149
Senior diet 68
Separation anxiety 61, 155

Sexual behavior 149
Sit 95
Size 16, 62
Skin problems 112
—auto-immune 113
—inherited 112
Snoring 22
Socialization 55
Socrates di Ponzano 11
Sottile, Michael 12
Squarcione 13
Standard 28, 138, 142
Stay 97
Stealing food 154
Sumerians 9
Tail 18
Tapeworm 128
Taste buds 68
Teresina della Casa Lazzarone 12
Thorndike, Dr. Edward 93
Thorndike's Theory of Learning 93
Threadworms 129
Tibetan Mastiff 9
Tick 122
Toxocara canis 127
Toys 45, 151
Tracheobronchitis 110
Training 57
—equipment 93
Traveling 75
Treats 93
Type 11
Uncinaria stenocephala **128**
United Kennel Club 140
United States 12
United States Neopolitan Mastiff Club 139
Unno 12
Ur 12
Uveitis 135
Vaccinations 109
Valeria della Grotta Azzurra 12
Veterinarian 53, 105, 107, 123, 127
Water 69
Weight 16
Whining 61
Whipworms 128
Working dog 23
World Dog Show 143
Zimbo della Zacchera 13

My Neapolitan Mastiff

PUT YOUR PUPPY'S FIRST PICTURE HERE

Dog's Name _____

Date _____ Photographer _____